# The Internet Interconnection Conundrum

# The Internet Interconnection Conundrum

## A Technology Policy Analysis of Service Provider Interconnection Issues

**Cameron I. Cooper**
**Joshua L Mindel**
**Douglas C. Sicker**

iUniverse, Inc.
New York  Lincoln  Shanghai

# The Internet Interconnection Conundrum
## A Technology Policy Analysis of Service Provider Interconnection Issues

iUniverse books may be ordered through booksellers or by contacting:

iUniverse
2021 Pine Lake Road, Suite 100
Lincoln, NE 68512
www.iuniverse.com
1-800-Authors (1-800-288-4677)

ISBN: 978-0-595-41307-2 (pbk)
ISBN: 978-0-595-85662-6 (ebk)

Printed in the United States of America

# CONTENTS

# LIST OF TABLES

# LIST OF FIGURES

# LIST OF ACRONYMS

| | |
|---|---|
| AIN | Advanced Intelligent Network |
| ANSI | American National Standards Institute |
| ARPA | Advance Research Projects Agency |
| ARPANET | Advance Research Projects Agency Network |
| AS | Autonomous System |
| ATIS | Alliance for Telecommunications Industry Solutions |
| ATM | Asynchronous Transfer Mode |
| BB | Bandwidth Broker |
| BGP | Border Gateway Protocol |
| CALEA | Communications Assistance for Law Enforcement Act |
| CARP | Cache Array Routing Protocol |
| CBT | Core-Based Tree |
| CC Docket | Common Carrier Docket |
| CLEC | Competitive Local Exchange Carrier |
| CMO | Committee Management Officer |
| CMRS | Commercial Mobile Radio Service |
| DARPA | Defense Advanced Research Project Agency |
| DBS | Direct Broadcast Satellite |
| DEN | Directory-Enabled Network |
| DHCP | Dynamic Host Configuration Protocol |
| DLEC | Data Local Exchange Carrier |
| DNS | Domain Name Service |
| DoJ | Department of Justice |
| DS | Digital Signal |
| DVMRP | Distance Vector Multicast Routing Protocol |
| EGP | Exterior Gateway Protocol |
| FACA | Federal Advisory Committee Act |
| FCC Rcd. | Federal Communications Commission Record |
| FCC | Federal Communications Commission |
| FR | Frame Relay |
| Gbps | Gigabits per second |

| | |
|---|---|
| GSA | General Services Administration |
| HTCP | Hyper Text Caching Protocol |
| ICMP | Internet Control Message Protocol |
| ICP | Internet Cache Protocol |
| IEEE | Institute of Electrical and Electronics Engineers |
| IETF | Internet Engineering Task Force |
| IGMP | Internet Group Message Protocol |
| IGRP | Interior Gateway Routing Protocol |
| ILEC | Incumbent Local Exchange Carrier |
| IM | Instant Messaging |
| IN | Intelligent Network |
| IP | Internet Protocol |
| IPDC | Internet Protocol Device Control |
| IPng | IP next generation |
| IPv4 | Internet Protocol version 4 |
| IPv6 | Internet Protocol version 6 |
| ISDN | Integrated Services Digital Network |
| ISO | International Organization for Standardization |
| ISP | Internet Service Provider |
| ITU | International Telecommunications Union |
| IXC | Interexchange Carrier |
| Kbps | Kilobits per second |
| LAN | Local Area Network |
| LDP | Label Distribution Protocol |
| LEC | Local Exchange Carrier |
| LNP | Local Number Portability |
| MAE-East | Metropolitan Area Exchange-East |
| MAE-West | Metropolitan Area Exchange-West |
| MBONE | Multicast Backbone |
| Mbps | Megabits per second |
| MFTP | Multicast File Transfer Protocol |
| MGCP | Media Gateway Control Protocol |
| MOSPF | Multicast Open Shortest Path First |
| MPLS | Multi Packet Label Switching |
| NAP | Network Access Point |
| NOI | Notice of Inquiry |
| NSF | National Science Foundation |
| NSFnet | National Science Foundation net |
| O&M | Operations and Maintenance |

| OPP | FCC's Office of Plans and Policy |
| OSI | Open Systems Interconnection |
| OSPF | Open Shortest Path First |
| PAC | Proxy Auto Configuration |
| PDU | Protocol Data Unit |
| PHB | Per-hop Behavior |
| PIM | Protocol Independent Protocol |
| PIM-DM | Protocol-Independent Multicast—Dense Mode |
| PIM-SM | Protocol-Independent Multicast—Sparse Mode |
| POTS | Plain Old Telephone Service |
| PSTN | Public Switched Telephone Network |
| QoS | Quality of Service |
| R&D | Research and Development |
| RBOC | Regional Bell Operating Company |
| RFC | Request for Comment |
| RIP | Routing Information Protocol |
| RMP | Reliable Multicast Protocol |
| RSVP | ReSerVation Protocol |
| RTCP | Real-Time Control Protocol |
| RTP | Real-Time Transport Protocol |
| SGCP | Simple Gateway Control Protocol |
| SIP | Session Initiation Protocol |
| SLA | Service Level Agreement |
| SLO | Service Level Objective |
| SLP | Service Location Protocol |
| SLS | Service Level Specification |
| SNA | Synchronous Network Architecture |
| SS7 | Signaling System 7 |
| T1 | Telecommunications Carrier 1 |
| Tbps | Terabits per second |
| TCA | Traffic Conditioning Agreement |
| TCP | Transmission Control Protocol |
| TIA | Telecommunications Industry Association |
| ToS | Type of Service |
| TPACP | Transparent Proxy Agent Control Protocol |
| UDP | User Datagram Protocol |
| UNE | Unbundled Network Element |
| URL | Uniform Resource Locator |
| vBNS | very high speed Backbone Network Service |

| VoIP | Voice over Internet Protocol |
|------|------------------------------|
| VPN | Virtual Private Network |
| WAN | Wide Area Network |
| WCCP | Web Cache Coordination Protocol |
| WPAD | Web Proxy Auto-Discovery Protocol |

# PREFACE

The original draft of this book was prepared during the summer of 1999, yet its primary message is still relevant today. Interconnection issues associated with Internet Protocol (IP) networks and applications are fundamentally different and more complex than that with which telecommunications legislation, regulation, and policy makers have previously had to grapple. The explanations and layered framework presented in this book are intended as a guide.

The reasons to publish this work in 2006 are twofold. First, it will serve as a published version of the layered model that has been referenced in the peer-reviewed telecommunications policy literature.[1] Second, it will broaden exposure to the interconnection analysis issues that relate to but are much broader than that described layered model. We foresee this as valuable material for the audience described in the following section.

In order to retain the spirit of the unpublished work, the authors have endeavored to minimally change the original work. The only alterations were made for the purposes of publication. It was decided, however, to retain the original citations (including Web references), some of which may no longer be viable. Readers interested in pursuing these references further are encouraged to contact the referenced organization (e.g., IETF, FCC, Level 3, and so on) for archival information.

---

1   For example, Richard S. Whitt, "A Horizontal Leap Forward: Formulating a New Communications Public Policy Framework Based on the Network Layers Model," *Fed. Comm. L. J.* 56, no. 587 (2004); M. Kende, "The Digital Handshake: Connecting Internet Backbones" (OPP Working Paper No. 32, Federal Communications Commission, 2000); D. Sicker and J. Mindel, "Refinements of a Layered Model for Telecommunications Policy," *Journal of Telecommunications and High Technology Law* 1, no. 1 (2002): 69–94; J. Mindel and D. Sicker, "Leveraging the EU regulatory framework to improve a layered policy model for U.S. telecommunications markets," *Telecommunications Policy* 30 (2006): 136–148.

## Who Should Read This Book

This book is published for telecommunications policy makers, analysts, business professionals, academics, and students who wish to better understand and evaluate Internet interconnection issues among network and Internet service providers. Students studying telecommunications policy and/or markets at the undergraduate or graduate level should be in a position to appreciate and critique the issues presented.

## Acknowledgments

The authors would like to express their appreciation to Dale Hatfield, former chief of the Office of Engineering and Technology (OET) at the Federal Communications Commission (FCC), and Robert Pepper, former chief of the Office of Plans and Policy (OPP) at the FCC, for their insight and the opportunity they provided for the three authors to brainstorm and draft this manuscript at the FCC during the summer of 1999.

The views expressed in this book are those of the authors and do not necessarily reflect the views of anyone at the FCC.

# 1

# INTRODUCTION

The emerging public packet-switched telecommunications infrastructure has significant implications for telecommunications policy in the United States and abroad. The existing legislative and regulatory frameworks were developed for a previous generation of telecommunications infrastructure and industry. Given the incongruity of policy and radically new infrastructure, the interconnection of emerging public telecommunications networks raises a number of unique and challenging policy questions. This book explores these questions from a technology perspective, highlighting in particular the implications of the new network architectures for interconnection policies. Rather than focusing on the technical details, this book explores the relationship of technology and policy.

In a competitive market with no dominant provider, providers are willing to interconnect their networks to capture the value associated with a larger pool of interconnected users and resources. Without interconnection, networks fragment, which prevents users from communicating readily. The value the user derives from being on the network increases as a function of the number of users on the network. Interconnection increases these network effects, and by extension, the positive network externalities (i.e., benefits) that users of the network reap.[2]

Interconnection policies, whether implemented as a result of market or government influences, are fundamental to ensuring interconnectivity of public networks provided by multiple competing firms. In general, public policy goals are met through a number of interdependent mechanisms, including market pressures, technological innovation, government regulation, and antitrust and other court rulings. Throughout much of telecommunications history, government regulation

---

2    The incentives to interconnect are a well-studied area; numerous publications are available on this subject. See the work of Economides, Nicholas, and Kende.

has been the primary mechanism for ensuring that public policy goals were met. However, the Telecommunications Act of 1996 requires the FCC to move toward a more market-driven approach. Making this transition requires that the present regulatory structure be streamlined to allow market mechanisms to operate, while ensuring that historic public policy goals continue to be met.

This book explores interconnection policies from the perspective of a competitive market environment. Devising interconnection policies for future packet networks presents a complex problem for the government. There is an overwhelming push not to apply regulatory obligations to the Internet, which raises the question, What is the Internet? Clarification of this issue is an important step toward ensuring that the Internet is not regulated. The authors believe that IP transport should be distinguished from the applications that *use* IP transport. In this context, applications include (1) intermediate applications, such as network signaling, multicasting, and caching; (2) end-user applications, such as user signaling, electronic mail, and Web browsing; and (3) content, such as Web pages and news sites. This boundary should not be perceived as indicating the need to regulate IP transport. Rather, it should be viewed as the logical separation of content from conduit. This boundary represents a logical line according to the services and players who provide these services. This book examines this boundary in terms of emerging technology implications for telecommunications policy and regulations.

One of the conundrums that the Internet presents is that of ensuring interconnection as we move away from specific mandates. Future interconnection policy must consider how to abstain from imposing interconnection obligations, while not allowing any single carrier to become dominant. There is little guiding precedent other than the outgrowth of the FCC's various Computer Inquiries and the existing peering and transit arrangements between Internet Service Providers (ISPs).[3] These latter arrangements have limited use in that they focus solely on packet exchange in a best-effort network. Such networks do not have quality-of-service

---

3    Computer Inquiry I (1966) distinguished between regulated communications and computers connecting to telephone lines. Computer Inquiry II (1976) defined basic and enhanced services. Basic service was defined as a pure transmission service offered by a regulated telecommunications carrier over a communications path that is virtually transparent in terms of its interaction with customer-supplied information. Enhanced service was defined as a service offered over common-carrier transmission facilities. This service employed computer-processing applications that modified the subscriber's transmitted information or involved subscriber interaction with stored information.

guarantees. We need a broader view of interconnection that considers the additional policy complexity introduced by the interconnection of IP transport networks used to provide integrated services based on applications requiring certain quality of service levels. This book seeks to provide policy insight by analyzing key architectural issues that bring about this complexity, including those identified in Table 1.1.

## Table 1.1 Key Architectural Issues That Bring About Policy Complexity

- Differentiated levels of service and quality of service
- Routing arrangements (peering and transit)
- Multicasting
- Signaling
- Caching
- Traffic exchange points

Our analysis is based on a distinction between the data delivery service provided by the Internet Protocol (IP) and the applications that use this data delivery service. IP provides the functionality needed to deliver a package of data from a source to a destination over multiple packet-switched networks.[4] *IP transport* is the term used to denote this data delivery function. From a policy and perhaps business perspective, this service is distinct from the applications that use the IP transport service, such as electronic mail, telephony, video streams, and so on. This distinction is less clear within the traditional voice world, where the transport was optimized for a specific application (voice). The Internet also introduces a newly expanded set of functions, referred to here as *intermediate* or *network-enabling applications.*[5] This includes functions such as caching and multicasting.

---

4    Other networks also provide this same functionality. For example, frame relay networks pass packages of data through multiswitched networks; therefore, frame relay is a transport service. The distinctions separating IP and frame relay transport are discussed in chapter 3.

5    Some might argue that these applications are actually transport functions; we address this issue in detail in chapter 5.

This book has been written for several audiences, including the policy makers, the technology industry, and those interested in the development of telecommunications policy. It acquaints the reader with the various IP technologies that will play a major role in future networks. It provides the industry with insight into interconnection policy issues important to the FCC, and it will hopefully encourage the industry to develop standards and deploy technologies that minimize regulatory intervention. At the same time, this book provides information to other individuals interested in developing sound interconnection policies for the emerging telecommunications infrastructure. It is not the intention of the authors to establish regulatory structures for the Internet; rather, it is to establish where regulation is not required.

Two points are worth mentioning at the outset. First, while this work considers interconnection issues relating to the Internet, the underlying policy principles are rather generic and can apply to various packet-based networks. Second, while this book does not focus specifically on content issues concerning packet networks, such as video, it is likely that this area will emerge as an important regulatory challenge. As traditional or new dominant players enter the content side of Internet programming, much of the traditional work done by the FCC will need to be reexamined in terms of the Internet. Here again, changes occurring in technology and the market may force the FCC and/or Congress to reexamine how best to proceed. The trick is how *not* to impose rules designed for monopoly carriers on emerging services and providers.

## 1.1   Overview of Book

Chapter 2 reviews existing telecommunications policy and the goals that underlie it. Chapter 3 emphasizes why IP interconnection is unique and worthy of this independent analysis. Chapters 4 and 5 describe and apply an analytical framework for examining interconnection relationships. Chapters 6 and 7 discuss the public policy implications of IP interconnection.

The Afterword brings this manuscript up to date. Specifically, we present a refined version of the layered model framework (published in 2002) that relates several current interconnection issues in the news to the framework.

Finally, the appendix provides a brief tutorial on relevant protocols and protocol standards that can serve as a primer for interested readers.

# 2

# TELECOMMUNICATIONS POLICY

The tremendous changes occurring in the national (and global) telecommunications infrastructure have broad-ranging implications for U.S. telecommunications policies. These policies refer to a set of public goals and a set of methods deemed most appropriate to achieve these goals.

In order to interpret the implications of emerging networks for telecommunications policy, we must first understand the goals upon which the policies are based. Depending on stakeholder perspectives, the relative importance of these policy goals may vary. Stakeholders include policy makers (such as Congress, the FCC, and state public utility commissions), industry players, academics, consumer groups, the public, and so on. Table 2.1 lists several important goals.

### Table 2.1 Sample Telecommunications Policy Goals

- Ubiquity of service availability
- Free flow of information
- Nondiscrimination in the carriage of information
- Reasonable pricing (e.g., cost-based prices, no monopoly rents)
- Efficient use of public resources (e.g., spectrum, rights-of-way)
- Investment
- Availability of advanced services (innovation)

In the broadest sense, the government has traditionally used three methods, or sets of tools, to achieve telecommunications policy goals:

- *Setting market rules to achieve economic goals.* For example, (1) managing accumulation of market power via merger reviews and antitrust proceedings, (2) requiring resale and unbundling to reduce the barriers to entry that new competitors face, (3) requiring that telecommunications carriers interconnect with all players to reduce barriers to entry, (4) regulating prices when market forces are absent due to perceived natural monopolies, and (5) ensuring separation to prevent a monopoly from subsidizing a competitive business segment with excess profits generated from a monopoly business segment.

- *Supporting societal goals.* For example, requiring that all telecommunications carriers pay into the Universal Service Fund to subsidize communications access for selected groups of U.S. residents and organizations.

- *Investment in public initiatives.* For example, by funding the National Science Foundation Net (NSFnet) backbone network (1985 to 1995), the government was investing in public initiatives (i.e., the education research infrastructure). This investment also encouraged innovation by providing a network infrastructure upon which new services could be developed, tested, and deployed.

## 2.1  Legislative Shift in Public Policy

Throughout most of this past century, the government has relied heavily on regulation to achieve telecommunications public goals. Regulatory policy strictly separated different modes of communications to ensure that (1) competitive sectors were not stifled by burdensome regulation and (2) existing monopolies could not be leveraged into competitive sectors in an effort to undermine competition.

It is well documented, however, that regulatory agencies are unable to keep pace with rapidly evolving markets and therefore can stifle the industry they intend to monitor.[6] Rather than attempt to develop new insight into this issue, we simply present (in Table 2.2) a general list of shortcomings associated with a regulatory approach to industry oversight.

---

6    T. J. Duesterberg and K. Gordon, *Competition and Deregulation in Telecommunications: The Case for a New Paradigm* (Washington DC: Brookings Institution Press, 1997).

## Table 2.2 Disadvantages of Regulation

- Regulators might be overly influenced by industry lobbyists (i.e., regulatory capture)
- Promise of public investment easy for incumbent
- Nonresponsiveness to technical change
- Insufficient/unknowledgeable staff at regulatory agency
- Difficulty in obtaining accurate industry information
- Vagueness of statutory standards
- Inadequate incentive for regulators to recognize new technology

The Communications Act of 1934, as updated by the Telecommunications Act of 1996[7] (hereafter referred to as the *Communications Act*), shows a significant policy shift, reflected in the rules under which telecommunications markets operate. The Communications Act directs the FCC to shift to a less regulatory environment. Part of this shift includes moving to a market approach rather than relying on the burdensome common-carrier policy now in place. Table 2.3 identifies several advantages of the market approach.

## Table 2.3 Advantages of Market Approach

- More rapid innovation
- Lower pricing of products and services
- Higher investment
- Increased deployment
- Increased employment
- Faster time to market
- Higher profits

Before market mechanisms can operate, however, there must be a sufficiently competitive market environment. There is hope that alternative players (and facilities)

---

7    *Telecommunications Act of 1996*, Public Law 104–104, 110 State (1996): 56. The 1996 Act amends the Communications Act of 1934, 47 U.S.C. §§ 151 et. seq.

will soon be available in adequate numbers to ensure reasonable levels of competition. The government continues to invest significant regulatory effort toward opening the Public Switched Telephone Network (PSTN) to enable competition.[8] Time will tell whether recent FCC efforts will improve this situation.

For interconnection in particular, FCC policy should ensure that interconnection is not destroyed or disabled by distortions in the market. Transitioning to a market-driven model is not a simple matter. It involves much more than dismissing the current regulatory framework and blindly relying on the market. A number of concerns surround interconnection in a market-based approach, the most prominent of which is the dominant control of an essential service. This is especially true now that the FCC has placed greater emphasis on reactive (i.e., ex-post) measures (such as enforcement of rules, contract law, and antitrust) and less emphasis on traditional proactive (i.e., ex-ante) regulatory measures. This shift may create a slow-to-respond process that can lead to market distortion. The trick will be to determine how to encourage interconnections while not imposing burdensome regulations on networks. One example of government intervention without regulation was the set of conditions that were applied by the EU and U.S. Department of Justice in approving the merger of MCI and WorldCom. As a condition of merger approval, MCI was required to divest its Internet business.

The divestiture was structured to include all assets, except for long-haul lines. It included the transfer of all of MCI's contracts with wholesale and retail customers for the provision of Internet backbone services, the transfer of all necessary employees to support the iMCI business being transferred, and all other necessary support arrangements to fulfill existing contractual obligations of the iMCI business. MCI/WorldCom was to refrain from soliciting or contracting to provide dedicated Internet access services for a specified period. MCI/WorldCom was also required to assign to Cable & Wireless iMCI's peering agreement with WorldCom and agree not to terminate that agreement for a period of five years. These conditions were imposed to ensure that the new competitor would be a significant player with the ability to compete effectively with MCI/WorldCom. It is important to note that these actions do not preclude MCI/WorldCom from eventually reaching a monopoly position. It is possible that in the future the market may tip, having MCI/WorldCom as the dominant player. However, if that

---

8    The *FCC First Report and Order* (FCC 96–325) that addresses interconnection between Local Exchange Carriers and Commercial Mobile Radio Service Providers is 737 pages.

does happen, it will be because the company outcompeted the other networks, not because it bought customers.[9]

## 2.2 Reshaping Policy to Meet Needs of Emerging Industry Structure and Infrastructure

The Communications Act is a significant step forward, but it may fall short of the legislative framework needed to oversee and guide the emerging telecommunications industry structure and infrastructure.

First, the Communications Act still addresses competition only among the traditional lines of communications—i.e., Local Exchange Carriers (LECs), Commercial Mobile Radio Service (CMRS), Interexchange Carriers (IXCs), and cable companies. The Communications Act provides little guidance for policies that will be needed to accommodate the evolving telecommunications infrastructure that is blurring the boundaries between industries. One cause of this blurring is that the *information services* sector of the marketplace has grown beyond being just a layer of services on top of telecommunications; it has become telecommunications itself. For example, national IP backbone service is considered an *information service* from a regulatory perspective, but one may argue that what an IP backbone provides is the "telecommunications," i.e., the "transmission, between or among points specified by the user, of information of the user's choosing, without change in the form or content of the information as sent and received," as taken from the Telecommunications Act of 1996.

Another shortcoming of the Communications Act is that it does not provide much-needed direction to industry, local and state regulators, and the public. Such a direction might provide a mechanism for cooperation, rather than penalizing industry participants after they violate some poorly articulated policy. Such a mechanism might include Title- (e.g., Title II, III, and VI)[10] independent guidelines for the interconnection of packet networks. Whatever role policy makers

---

9    C. Robinson, "Network Effects in Telecommunications Mergers: MCI WorldCom Merger: Protecting the Future of the Internet" (Director of Operations and Merger Enforcement, Antitrust Division, U.S. Department of Justice. Presented to the Practicing Law Institute in San Francisco, August 1999).

10   Title II refers to common carriers. Title III refers to radio-based services. Title VI refers to cable communications.

assume, it is essential that this involvement takes a forward-looking perspective and departs from the existing title-specific regulation.

It is important to note that this policy direction need not imply regulation; policy and regulation are not equivalent. Regulation is but one of several mechanisms used to implement telecommunications policy. Without developing a coherent telecommunications policy that ensures the achievement of its goals, it is no more sensible to proclaim "no Internet regulation" than it is to proclaim "Internet regulation."[11, 12]

We believe that the FCC is appropriately "reluctant to impose any regulatory mandate that relies on the persistence of a particular market model or market structure."[13] The intent of this book is to provide insight into issues that are relevant to developing a sound interconnection policy for the emerging IP network infrastructure. A sound policy must reflect the uniqueness of the targeted market and not simply carry over existing regulations.

The market dynamics of the Internet are quite different from the previous generation of industry and infrastructure. Many of the existing regulations are service oriented and focus on monopolies that, arguably, were developed with the government's assistance.[14] The Internet has been very strongly influenced by government-motivated activity, yet it has emerged as the basis for the new telecommunications infrastructure in a fiercely competitive market. Consider the following examples:

---

11   It is a common misconception that the Internet is completely unregulated today, when in fact parts of it *are* regulated. For example, many of the underlying telecommunications circuits upon which the Internet runs are provided by regulated telecommunications service providers.

12   A related misconception is that the FCC has no authority with respect to information service providers, such as ISPs. The FCC explicitly acted on behalf of ISPs in its decisions to exempt ISPs from access charges. Source: Jason Oxman, "The FCC and the Unregulation of the Internet" (OPP WP July 31, 1999).

13   "Report to Congress in the Matter of Federal-State Joint Board on Universal Service" (April 10, 1998).

14   The Willis-Graham Act of 1921 removed obstacles to unification of telephone companies by exempting telephone companies from the Sherman Act.

- The Advance Research Projects Agency (ARPA) sent out the first request for proposals for the ARPA Network (ARPANET) in 1965. ARPANET was commissioned by the Department of Defense for research on networking in 1969.[15]

- The National Science Foundation (NSF) funded establishment of NSFnet in 1986 to provide universities with high-speed network connections.[16]

- The NSF created InterNIC to provide directory and database services (via a contract awarded to AT&T), registration services (via a contract awarded to Network Solutions, Inc.), and information services (via a CERFnet contract to General Atomics).[17]

- Originally, four network access points (NAPs)—in New York, Washington DC, Chicago, and San Francisco—were created and supported by the NSF as part of the transition from the original U.S. government-financed Internet to a commercially operated Internet.

- The very high speed Backbone Network Service (vBNS) and Internet2 are NSF-funded research networks that were initiated once the original NSFnet was decommissioned in 1995.

Equally important, the Internet defies service-oriented definitions—other than transport characteristics—because of its ability to enable both existing and unforeseen services. The Internet uses IP "to deliver a package of bits (an Internet datagram) from a source to a destination over an interconnected system of networks."[18] IP transport refers to the connectionless data delivery service offered by IP networks. An IP backbone network is an example of an IP transport network. For the purposes of this book, operations and maintenance (O&M) activities of IP transport services are included in the definition of IP transport services.

---

15   Hobbes' Internet Timeline v4.2, http://www.isoc.org/zakon/Internet/History/HIT.html.

16   Hobbes' Internet Timeline v4.2, http://www.isoc.org/zakon/Internet/History/HIT.html.

17   Hobbes' Internet Timeline v4.2, http://www.isoc.org/zakon/Internet/History/HIT.html.

18   J. Postel, "Internet Protocol: DARPA [Defense Advanced Research Project Agency] Internet Program Protocol Specification" (USC/Information Sciences Institute, IETF RFC [Request for Comment] 791, September 1981).

Updating routing tables and providing Quality of Service (QoS) are two typical examples of such O&M activities. Electronic mail, IP telephony, Web browsing, instant messaging, and directory services are all examples of applications that *use* the IP transport service but are not *part* of the IP transport service.

Distinguishing transport services from the applications that *use* transport services will help policy makers focus on the particular market dynamics that are important to interconnection policy. The risk of not taking this approach is that policy initiatives may be ambiguous, ineffective, and potentially detrimental. It is important to emphasize that this distinction is not limited to IP. Consider ISP markets, for example:

- The ISP market is a general term that encompasses provision-of-access services that constitute distinct market segments (e.g., data delivery, telephony signaling, caching, electronic mail).

- ISP markets are considered to be competitive today.

- ISPs reap network externalities from interconnection with other ISPs.

- Current law does not mandate interconnection of ISPs.

In this market context, what interconnection policies are appropriate for the emerging transport networks, application providers, and content providers? The policy needs to enable firms to take advantage of demand and supply-side economies of scale, yet also ensure that artificial barriers to entry do not limit competition. Chapter 3 delves into the unique and rich functionality offered by the emerging telecommunications infrastructure. The chapter also takes us one step closer to developing policy insights for interconnection.

# 3

# UNIQUENESS OF INTERCONNECTION

Interconnection in the emerging IP network context is unique in several respects. First, as compared to interconnection in the circuit-switched industry/infrastructure context, there is a far richer set of engineering and market structure issues to address. Sections 3.1 through 3.4 identify and describe a representative set of these issues.

From an engineering perspective, the interconnection of Plain Old Telephone Service (POTS) networks involve far fewer issues than future IP networks. Policies for circuit-switched public networks have benefited greatly from various corporate, national, and international standards efforts throughout most of the past century. If we consider Frame Relay (FR) and Asynchronous Transfer Mode (ATM) networks—both regulated as telecommunications services—we find that there are few intercarrier interconnection agreements implemented in the market.[19] The need for this intercarrier relationship was recognized early, and standards exist.[20] Virtual circuits within ATM and FR clouds generally originate and terminate within a given provider's network. The question is whether this lack of interconnection is due to (1) a lack of demand, (2) a carrier exerting market dominance, (3) a lack of effective government interconnection policies, or (4) some other factor. This lack of ATM/FR interconnection raises the obvious

---

19  Some providers of FR service purchased leased lines in order to provide the transport facilities required to offer their frame service. For example, this is how many FR networks provide international services. Also, where prohibited by interlata restrictions, Regional Bell Operating Companies (RBOCs) must hand off traffic.

20  See http://www.mfaforum.org/ftp/pub/approved-specs/af-bici-0068.000.pdf.

question: How might interconnection develop in an integrated-service Internet? Are these networks or markets so fundamentally different that this single-carrier network syndrome will not extend to IP, or is this a precursor of things to come? With the increasing likelihood that voice will be carried over IP, interconnection between networks will become increasingly more important. Lessons could likely be learned by considering the early-segmented telephony market.

The second respect with which interconnection is unique is that, viewed as a regulatory obligation, it has little similarity with other regulatory obligations triggered by existing regulatory classifications (e.g., telecommunications service provider). The grouping of regulatory obligations is a result of historic and regulatory convenience rather than any inherent similarity or relationship between interconnection, Universal Service Fund, and nondiscrimination issues.

In a competitive market with no dominant provider, providers are willing to interconnect their networks to capture the value associated with a larger pool of interconnected users and resources. Without interconnection, networks fragment, preventing users from communicating readily. The value that the user derives from being on the network increases as a function of the number of users on the network. This value of interconnectivity is known as *network externality*.[21] Therefore, when considering interconnection policies for the emerging telecommunications infrastructure, it is appropriate to separately analyze interconnection without being bogged down by the potential implications for other policy obligations. The other obligations are important, but they are beyond the scope of this book.

This book focuses on the engineering and market aspects of interconnection. Sections 3.1 through 3.4 address the fundamental differences between interconnection in an IP environment and interconnection in the POTS PSTN. We also extend this comparison to the future Internet, where QoS and other applications further these differences. Interconnection in the Internet differs with the PSTN from the perspective of industry, regulation, network architecture, bandwidth, signaling, and more. The intention of this chapter is to highlight the differences, not to exhaustively explore this topic.

---

21    The incentives to interconnect are a well-studied area; numerous publications are available on this subject. See Economides, Nicholas, and Kende.

## 3.1  Regulation Is Different

The Communications Act is designed to "promote competition and reduce regulation" while encouraging "the rapid deployment of new telecommunications technologies." Central to these objectives is the need to address the local telephone monopolies. The Communications Act defines the initial requirements of network interconnection and unbundling for all telecommunications carriers as follows:

- Section 201 of the Communications Act mandates certain interconnection obligations.

- Section 251(a) of the Communications Act mandates very general interconnection obligations on all carriers.

- Section 251(b) imposes certain interconnection obligations on all LECs—both Competitive LECs (CLECs) and Incumbent LECs (ILECs).

- Sections 251(c) and 271 mandate very specific interconnection and unbundling obligations for all RBOCs.

- Section 256 defines interconnectivity of the public telecommunication network as "the ability of two or more public telecommunications networks used to provide telecommunication service to communicate and exchange information without degradation and to interact in concert with one another."

ISPs are not classified as telecommunications carriers and are therefore not subject to these interconnection obligations. Figure 3.1 shows a regulatory continuum for communications-related services. At the far left, you have POTS and the PSTN. These services have a long history of regulation. Just to the left side of the vertical boundary, you have technologies that provide a data transmission or transport service. Just to the right of the boundary, under Information Service, you have another data transport service called IP. The difference in how these services are defined has led to companies implementing various arbitrage models.

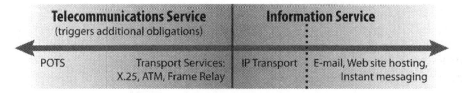

**Figure 3.1 Regulatory Distinctions**

This creates the possibility that dominant service providers may exploit these discrepancies in a manner that circumvents regulatory obligations established to prevent such market dominance.

## 3.2  Industry Is Different

For the most part, the communications industry has been comprised of a few highly regulated players providing a single service, such as a voice channel or cable network. Since the advent of the Internet and passage of the Telecommunications Act of 1996, however, multitudes of players and services have entered the market. There is now vibrant competition for transport services and services extending well beyond simple transport. For telecommunications policy, the emerging market structure can be viewed as consisting of providers of IP transport services and providers of applications that use the IP transport services. Transport providers in this case include access as well as backbone providers, and application providers include content as well as applications. These industry sectors are distinguishable in terms of economies of scale, market characteristics, and sources of competitive advantage. Many of the value-added services of the future will result from the integration of IP transport and applications services. The varied service capabilities of transport networks have resulted in a number of differing performance requirements. Examples include file transfer, e-mail, streamed services, push media, distance learning, and groupware. Time and bandwidth-sensitive services require a certain level of cooperation and coordination between the two industry sectors, despite differences in market characteristics and sources of competitive advantage. Real-time interactive services, such as VoIP or interactive video, have far more stringent latency and jitter requirements than do streaming or data-oriented services.

Cooperation and coordination also become more difficult with the number of players involved. In each of the respective sectors, the number of providers has exploded due to the commercialization of the Internet and the deregulation of the telecommunications industry. One indicator of growth is that the number of registered IP transport networks climbed from hundreds in the 1980s to millions in the late 1990s. While the numbers are impressive, it is important to note that only those IP transport networks providing a public transport service (about eight thousand ISPs in 1999) are within the scope (or purview) of the interconnection issues we address in this book. [22] The other IP networks are private networks that exist to support the operation of an organization. Only a handful of these players,

---

22   *Boardwatch Magazine*, Spring 1999.

though, make up roughly 90 percent of that market. Regulators should recognize and closely monitor this concentrated market.

Within the IP transport sector, the FCC has distinguished between transmission links, which are considered a telecommunications service, and IP packet-switching, which is considered an information service. Most regulatory obligations are placed on companies providing transmission links. Few obligations are placed on the providers of IP packet-switched networks and providers of applications that rely on these networks. Competitively, there is little incentive for these providers to coordinate with their competitors to provide end-to-end service guarantees. They would rather horizontally integrate in order to expand their reach. This would allow them to offer service guarantees over a larger geographical area (e.g., AT&T/TCI and @Home, AOL and Direct Broadcast Satellite [DBS], AOL and TW).

At a certain level, the relationship of ILECs to IXCs can be compared to that of ISPs to backbone providers. ILECs rely on the IXCs to carry traffic beyond the local network, just as ISPs rely on backbone providers to carry traffic beyond the local network. However, this only goes so far because the regulatory, business, and architectural models differ significantly. For example, IXCs do not pass traffic to other IXCs as backbone providers might. In fact, an Internet connection might involve many backbone networks. An argument might be made that the additional complexity that the Internet brings in terms of the number of interceding networks furthers the problem of end-to-end service guarantees.

It is incumbent upon the FCC to find ways to ensure the successful deployment of new services, given the current and emerging market structure. In a deregulatory environment, this will likely require a certain amount of creative nonregulatory action on the part of the FCC.

## 3.3  Applications Are Different

Voice is really the application of the PSTN. By contrast, the Internet can support an immense number of applications. This difference is significant to interconnection policy because of the type of applications that must be interconnected, the rates and QoS demands of these applications, and the players involved in the interconnection. In other words, Internet applications place unique demands on the transport architecture, likely including more complex interconnection relationships. This is particularly the case as we move to an Internet that provides real-time services.

## Table 3.1 Application Distinctions

|  | Voice (PSTN) | Current IP Infrastructure | Future IP Infrastructure |
|---|---|---|---|
| Applications | Voice, low-speed data | Data, low-grade voice | Data, high-quality voice and video, etc. |
| Rate | Low (Fixed) | Variable | Variable |
| Location of control | Centralized | Decentralized | Both |
| Integration of transport and application | Combined | Separate | Both |

## 3.4 Architecture Is Different

To examine network architectures, we need to consider the protocols underlying the architecture. We can make use of these protocols to conceptualize the structure and complexity of IP interconnection.[23] The various layers of the IP stack each represent a point of interconnection to consider. This section considers these points in terms of the functionality that they provide. Interconnection will or may need to occur at a physical, data link, network, transport, control, and/or application level. For example, interconnection must include the ability for applications to interoperate. Instant messaging (IM) is an obvious example of this type of interconnection. For users to exchange messages, IM applications on one IM platform must be able to interconnect (and interoperate) with IM applications on other platforms. It is important to recognize that the PSTN does not present the same level of complexity in terms of layers of interconnection. A model that considers the various layers will take into account this complexity and the incentives or disincentives behind future interconnection agreements. This layered approach could be useful for examining a variety of issues presently before the FCC, such as cable open access and Internet peering.

In numerous dimensions, the architectures of PSTN and IP networks are different. It is precisely these differences that make it difficult to define interconnection policies for IP transport networks. Many of these architectural differences are a matter of the applications supported by the Internet. A quick review of fundamental architectural differences is provided in this section. This review will pro-

---

23    The appendix provides a tutorial on protocols.

vide a useful perspective for the analyses of IP interconnection elements provided in chapter 5. The architectural aspects listed in Table 3.2 are described in the text that follows.

**Table 3.2 Architectural Aspects Compared**

- Differentiated levels and QoS
- Routing arrangements (peering and transit)
- Multicasting
- Signaling
- Caching
- Traffic exchange points

Other aspects, such as directory services, network management, billing, and application control, do exist but are the subject of further study.

## 3.4.1  Differentiated Levels of Service and QoS

To better understand the notion of QoS, it is helpful to consider the problems that a person might experience when traveling for an important business meeting.

> Julie calls her travel agent to book a flight to Pittsburgh. Her agent finds two flights available; one is a nonstop flight to Pittsburgh, the other has a two-hour stopover in Chicago. While the nonstop flight costs twice as much, it gets Julie to Pittsburgh in two hours, whereas the other flight takes more than four hours to complete. Since these are last-minute travel plans and Julie has an important meeting to attend, she chooses to pay the extra money for the flight that will get her there in time for the meeting. Here Julie decides that she is willing to pay extra for a flight that gets her to her desired destination on time. In this way, she is willing to pay more for a service (the flight) of higher quality (less delay).

This scenario is analogous to QoS in packet-switched networks, where a user decides that the packets they are sending or receiving should not experience excessive delay traveling through the network. The user is willing to pay the network provider more for that higher level of service. A user's willingness to pay for this higher level of service is likely dependent on the applications that he or she is using. If the user is running a telephony service, then the delay traveling through the network must be minimized or the telephone service will be impaired.

All networks, regardless of the technology, provide a level of service and a quality of service. The level of service and associated quality define the characteristics that a user of this network can expect in terms of bandwidth, delay characteristics, availability, reliability, and so on. Table 3.3 provides a comparison of levels and qualities of service provided by PSTN and IP transport networks.

### Table 3.3 Service Quality Distinctions

| PSTN | IP Transport Network |
|---|---|
| • Bandwidth utilized is fixed at around 4 KHz. | • For best-effort level of service, bandwidth utilized is dynamic due to bursty nature of traffic. |
| • Switched network design is based on decades of observation and traffic modeling. | • QoS refers to level of service differentiated from that of current best-effort level of service. |
| • QoS refers to blocking probability, trouble ticket response times, and other aspects of ILEC arrangements. | • Differentiated levels of service implies bandwidth and delay characteristics are more controlled than in best-effort service. |
| • QoS for transmission is guaranteed once the call is placed by dedicating the network resources for the duration of the call. | • Technology to provide intradomain and interdomain QoS is not mature (e.g., DiffServ, RSVP/IntServ).[24] |
| | • Circuit-switched traffic models do not work well for packet-switched networks. |
| • Technologies to provide QoS are mature. | • Packet-switched traffic modeling for different levels of service is not yet well understood. |
| • Voice is dependent on high QoS. | • Many Internet applications do not demand QoS. |

---

24   Technology in this context includes not only the capability to guarantee a level of service, but also the usage of accounting and monitoring tools needed to accommodate the economic and management aspects of interdomain (i.e., provider-to-provider) QoS.

## 3.4.2   Routing

To better understand the notion of routing, it is helpful to consider the railroad industry. While this is not a particularly timely example, it does provide the user with an illustrative model.

> Railroads were once regional in their footprint; in other words, they may have served only discrete areas of the country. To move freight across the country, it was therefore necessary to switch between several railroads. This function was provided at railroad switching yards. Various railroads built tracks from their rail systems to railroad-switching yards. In order to move freight from New York to Kansas City, the company would first have to decide how to move it through its system of rails. First the company had to know what tracks were busy, what tracks were under repair, and what was the best route to the switching yard. This would allow the railroad to develop a route through its rail system to efficiently move its freight. At the switching yard, the various railroad companies would agree upon how to exchange boxcars so that they could reach the required destinations. This took the form of contacts identifying what cars would be delivered to what location, when they would be delivered, and how much this would cost.

This is analogous to what happens with routing and the exchange of packets in the Internet. Routing is the process of determining how best to move through the network, and the traffic points are where the actual exchange of packets and routing information occurs. All switched networks, regardless of the technology, entail routing arrangements to exchange information between originator and recipient. Table 3.4 provides a comparison of routing provided by PSTN and IP transport networks.

## Table 3.4 Routing Distinctions

| PSTN | IP Transport Network |
|---|---|
| • Path is selected at call setup and maintained for duration of call.<br><br>• Routes are maintained within and between carriers.<br><br>• All networks provide interconnection—and are regulated to do so.<br><br>• Users may designate both access (i.e., LECs) and long distance providers that they wish to use.<br><br>• FCC mandates interconnection but not the exchange of routing data.<br><br>• The routes are established well in advance. | • For best-effort level of service, route is established on a packet-by-packet basis.<br><br>• For a virtual circuit, route is established at call setup and maintained for duration of call.<br><br>• Routers implementing routing algorithms (such as border gateway protocol) establish routes.<br><br>• Routing between network providers is done via peering or transit agreements.<br><br>• Peering is arrangement in which packets are exchanged between providers without settlement.<br><br>• Transit implies that one network pays another for interconnection and essentially becomes a customer of that network.<br><br>• Users designate access providers (i.e., LECs and ISPs) but do not designate backbone providers (this choice is left to the ISP via routing arrangements), unless provided as dedicated access from backbone. |

### 3.4.2.1   Financial Transactions for Exchanging Traffic

Sending traffic to a competitor's network, or receiving traffic from a competitor's network, incurs a financial or opportunity cost. As such, all interconnection arrangements entail a financial arrangement between providers. The arrangement may be as simple as "no fees need to be exchanged," or they may be far more complex. For the PSTN and current best-effort IP services, the following comparison can be made.

## Table 3.5 Financial Remuneration Distinctions

| PSTN | IP Transport Network | IP Content/Application Service |
| --- | --- | --- |
| • Reciprocal compensation is the payment made from one carrier to another for carriage of traffic.<br><br>• Customer pays for transport/application. | • Peering implies "settlement-free" or "bill-and-keep" or "send-keep-all" arrangement in which each party bills its own customers only for the origination of traffic and does not pay the other party for terminating this traffic.<br><br>• Transit implies that one network pays another for interconnection and essentially becomes a customer of that network. | • This service provider is typically a customer of a transport provider.<br><br>• May pay transport provider or other IP content provider significant sums for "shelf space" on a portal or for "shelf space" on a caching server.<br><br>• Consumer pays IP content/application service provider. |

Interconnection of IP networks that employ QoS is more complex than interconnection between best-effort networks. This is because of the signaling required to request and accept network connections with specific performance guarantees. These guarantees enable the use of end-user applications that are highly sensitive to the available bandwidth and delay in the network (e.g., telephony and video playback).

Interconnection agreements for provider-to-provider QoS will likely take the form of Service Level Agreements (SLAs), rather than the relatively simple arrangements that are commonly used today (i.e., peering and transit). SLAs will likely specify a characterization of the network service (e.g., minimum bandwidth, maximum latency, and maximum jitter), settlements, measurement methods, traffic admission conditions, and so on.

### 3.4.3  Multicasting

To better understand the notion of multicasting, it is helpful to consider how a national newspaper distributes its papers to all the cities around the country in a timely and efficient manner.

> One could imagine that all the copies of the Wall Street Journal are printed at one location and then shipped overnight across the country to subscribers and newsstands. This would result in millions of copies of newspapers being shipped all over the country from one location—an incredibly expensive and inefficient process. To get around this problem, national newspapers make use of regional printing presses located throughout the country. The company transmits a copy of the paper to the regional printing press, which then prints copies for distribution in that region. This approach reduces the need to ship individual copies the entire way to the destination, thereby saving time and money and improving efficiency.

This newspaper distribution mechanism is analogous to Internet multicasting. Consider what would happen if an Internet designed to transmit a live audio feed of a popular musical group did not use multicasting. A huge number of fans would request this audio feed from this site. Since the Internet sends individual packets to each requesting site, there would be a significant increase in traffic, resulting in congestion and delay. To solve this problem, the Internet has a multicast mode. This allows a single packet to travel through the network to a "regional" point in the network, where the packet is replicated and then distributed to the destinations.

Multicasting attempts to mirror the capabilities of a broadcast medium onto what has traditionally been a nonbroadcast medium. Internet multicasting will make possible a range of new services. These services promise to add a whole new dimension to communications service. Multicasting and the resultant services will be discussed further in chapter 5. The important point to make here, however, is that the concept of multicasting is predominantly an IP networking technology. An adequate parallel to multicast does not exist within the POTS PSTN. Multicast is designed to limit the bandwidth necessary to provide one-to-many, many-to-many, and many-to-one communications on a commercial scale. While these communication modes are available within POTS PSTN (e.g., conference calling and voice broadcast services), they are more often than not provided via replicated unicast, which differs significantly from multicast. Table 3.6 provides a comparison of multicasting provided by POTS PSTN and IP networks.

**Table 3.6 Multicasting Distinctions**

| POTS PSTN | IP Application Service (that uses IP transport service) |
|---|---|
| • Replicated unicast (not real multicast). | • Multicast is provided via multicast protocols and any of a number of routing protocols (e.g., PIM-SM, CBT, DVMRP, MOSPF).[25] |

## 3.4.4 Signaling

To better understand the notion of signaling, it is helpful to consider how the telephone system operated at the turn of the century.

> Placing a call once required a human operator to patch through the connections from the calling party to the called party. For example, if a person were trying to call a friend who lived a few blocks away, she would first contact the operator at the local telephone office. The operator would ask for the number that the caller was trying to reach. Since this number was served out of the same office, the operator could complete the call herself. The operator would check to see whether the called party was available. If the line was not busy, the operator would ring the called party's phone. When the called party answered, the operator would patch the call back to the calling party. When the call ended, the operator would tear down the connection.

This process of setting up and tearing down calls defines much of what makes up signaling. This signaling has gone through several evolutionary phases and is now done by computers.

To provide a service such as telephony, a certain amount of signaling must occur across a network. This signaling entails the exchange of control information between providers and/or users. Signaling in the Internet may develop in a manner unlike signaling in the PSTN. The development of new signaling protocols will most likely alter how a service is provisioned and who participates in that provisioning. The present telephone network centralizes control within the carrier's network, causing difficulty in the timely provision of new services. The Internet

---

25   These acronyms and corresponding technologies are discussed in section 5.3, Multicasting.

model allows service control to migrate to the edge of the network, enabling users to deploy new services in a timely and competitive manner.

**Figure 3.2 Intelligence in the Network**

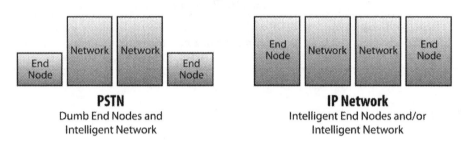

**PSTN**
Dumb End Nodes and
Intelligent Network

**IP Network**
Intelligent End Nodes and/or
Intelligent Network

Table 3.7 provides a comparison of signaling in PSTN and IP networks.

**Table 3.7 Signaling Distinctions**

| PSTN | IP Application Service |
|---|---|
| • Separate networks for content and signaling. | • Single network for both content and signaling. |
| • The transport network transmits content, whereas the control network transmits signaling. | • Signaling intelligence may lie in network or in end nodes. |
| • The content is a single type of application (voice), so interconnection policies need not interpret the data stream. | • Multiple evolving standards (e.g., MGCP, H.323, SIP).[26] |
| • Signaling intelligence lies in network; end nodes are assumed to be relatively dumb. | |
| • Mature standards. | |

---

26   These acronyms and corresponding technologies are discussed in section 5.4, Signaling.

## 3.4.5  Caching

To better understand the notion of caching, it is helpful to consider the national library system.

> A reader can travel to the Library of Congress to look for a copy of a particular book or go to his local library. Other people in the reader's town can also go to the library and look at that same book. As we all know, a library provides the public with free access to books, reference material, magazines, and online content. In this way, the book serves as a local copy of information available for everyone in a certain area to access. This local copy saves both time in accessing the information and money in not having to travel long distances to obtain the information. This is similar to what caching provides in the Internet. Caches are copies of Web pages that are stores closer to the user. The details of where and how caching occurs are explained in the following section.

As with multicasting, caching is predominantly an IP networking concept that is designed to conserve bandwidth by bringing data closer to the edges of the network with a minimum amount of replication. Both technologies are based upon the notion that there will be a simultaneous demand for certain services. Thus, only a single copy needs to be sent across the entire network. Servers at the edge of the network can then replicate the information as needed for their clients. Caching will be discussed in more detail in chapter 5.

### Table 3.8 Caching Distinction

| POTS PSTN | IP Application Service (that uses IP transport service) |
|---|---|
| • Caching does not exist. | • Caching is provided via a number of standards (e.g., HTCP, CARP, WCCP, SOCKS).[27] |

## 3.4.6  Traffic Exchange Points

The mix of firms participating in the provision of PSTN and IP networks is quite different. This mix has direct implications for the places at which competitive net-

---

27  These acronyms and corresponding technologies are discussed in section 5.5 Caching.

works are interconnected and thus for the topology of the overall interconnected network infrastructure. There is a fundamental difference between PSTN and IP exchange points. Table 3.9 highlights these differences.

### Table 3.9 Exchange Point Distinctions

| PSTN | IP Transport Network |
|---|---|
| • Traffic exchange points provided by carriers only; however, neutral or independent bandwidth trading markets of voice minutes is emerging.<br><br>• Service providers at the exchange points include (a) transport (telecommunications circuit) providers and (b) telephone exchange service (telephony) providers. | • Traffic exchanges (e.g., Metropolitan Area Exchange-East [MAE-E]) may be provided by a carrier (e.g., MCI WorldCom) or by a neutral or independent party that provides connectivity only.<br><br>• Service providers at the exchange points include (a) transport providers and (b) application providers, including intermediate services (e.g., signaling and caching), end-user services (e.g., electronic mail and Web hosting.), and content services (e.g., news sites). |

One similarity in traffic exchange points is that in both the PSTN and IP contexts, both transport providers and application providers interconnect at the traffic exchange points.

### 3.4.7  Other Services

Other services that differentiate interconnection in the Internet from the PSTN include directory services, network management, and billing. We do not discuss these services or functions in this book.

It should be clear from the previous examples that interconnection in the Internet is fundamentally different from interconnection in the PSTN, particularly as we move toward the provision of guaranteed services (QoS).

# 4

# FRAMEWORK FOR INTERCONNECTION

We have developed a conceptual framework with which to evaluate aspects of IP interconnection. This analysis addresses best-effort networks that are currently available, as well as QoS networks that are expected to become an integral component of the emerging telecommunications infrastructure. The framework provides a structure within which interconnection issues can be systematically identified and interpreted by distinguishing between IP transport services and applications that use these transport services. *Applications* refers to intermediate applications (e.g., multicasting), end-user applications (e.g., e-mail), and content services (e.g., news). The framework consists of relationships among the service provider types listed in Table 4.1.

**Table 4.1 Types of Service Providers Addressed in Framework**

| Service Provider Type | Explanation |
|---|---|
| Providers of IP Transport Services | Includes both best-effort and QoS services. These may include network operators, NAP operators, and GigaPOPs.[28] |
| Providers of Telecommunications Services | As defined in the Communications Act of 1934 (as amended by the Telecommunications Act of 1996). |

---

28  A GigaPOP, unlike a NAP, is a layer-three interconnection point that allows for aggregation of resources and access to services in a cost-effective manner.

| Service Provider Type | Explanation |
|---|---|
| Providers of Applications Services | Applications rely on underlying IP transport services. As discussed previously, this provider type includes (1) providers of content, (2) providers of intermediate services, such as multicasting and caching, and (3) providers of enduser applications, such as electronic mail and Web hosting |

One could argue that the three subcategories under Providers of Applications Services are distinct and should be viewed as such; however, this broad categorization is sufficient for this description of the framework. The point here is to *distinguish between the provision of a data delivery service and the entities that use the data delivery service.* The specific interconnection differences that arise for each of these three subcategories are brought out and addressed in detail when the framework is applied to an architectural issue (e.g., caching) in chapter 5.

While the relationship of software providers and consumers to the three identified provider types is crucial to the deployment and use of the infrastructure, it is not crucial to this interconnection analysis. Outside of Section 255 (Disability) and Communications Assistance for Law Enforcement Act (CALEA) concerns, software developers are not subject to telecommunications policy today. Provision of services tends to be of concern, rather than the providers of the service building block. Consumer benefits and costs are central motivating factors in telecommunications policy, but since they are not directly associated with interconnection of provider networks, they are also beyond the scope of this interconnection analysis.

The relationships that we deem most important to telecommunications interconnection policy are explained in Table 4.2.

### Table 4.2 Relationships in the Framework

| Short Name | Explanation |
|---|---|
| Relationship A | IP Transport Provider to IP Transport Provider |
| Relationship B | IP Transport Provider to Application Service Provider |
| Relationship C | Application Service Provider to Application Service Provider |
| Relationship D | Internet to Telecommunications Service Provider |

Table 4.2 shows these four interconnection relationships. The first three relationships (A, B, and C) are between providers of the emerging IP infrastructure. The fourth (D) is between a provider of the IP infrastructure and a provider within the legacy PSTN infrastructure.

For the emerging IP infrastructure, the figure shows both the conceptual (simplified) protocol stack and hypothetical network topologies that may be employed by providers. From a telecommunications policy perspective, this book focuses on the layers indicated. The IP transport service entails both access and transport networks. An IP transport provider will use applications on its network, but it also might offer the transport service to the public for a fee. Similarly, a caching provider will employ an Intranet to interconnect its caches and to connect its caches to the public IP transport network. Since it offers the caching service to the public for a fee, caching is the service of interest, not its Intranet.

For the legacy PSTN infrastructure, the figure shows telecommunications services to the right of the dotted line. Services that would be considered application services in an IP context (e.g., Signaling System 7 [SS7]/Intelligent Network [IN] and directory services) are to the left of the dotted line. In legacy PSTN regulation, both are considered *telecommunications services* and are therefore labeled as such in the figure.

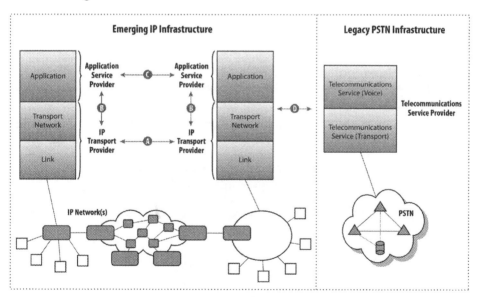

**Figure 4.1 Framework for Provider Relationships**

A fifth relationship could be included to reflect the relationship between transport service providers in the emerging IP infrastructure and in the legacy PSTN infrastructure. An example of this relationship is that of an ISP using telecommunications circuits of an ILEC. This relationship is not addressed in this book for several reasons: (1) it is already widely in place today, (2) there is already a regulatory framework in place today, and (3) it is not central to the IP interconnection architectural issues that are analyzed in this book.

## 4.1    (Relationship A) IP Transport Provider to IP Transport Provider

These relationships establish the interconnected IP transport infrastructure. The relationships are typified by the peering and transit arrangements for traffic exchange that exist. A peering arrangement is one in which two networks agree to exchange each other's traffic for free. A transit arrangement is distinct in that one party pays another for carrying its traffic. Tier 1 providers, or the largest backbone network providers, typically engage in peering arrangements with one another, while service providers with less traffic (and/or less market power) enter into agreements with them to carry traffic.[29, 30] Application services that these same providers may provide (such as EarthLink's e-mail service) are not included in the IP-transport-provider-to-IP-transport-provider relationship. Interdomain QoS interconnection will fall into this relationship category as well.

## 4.2    (Relationship B) IP Transport Provider to Application Service Provider

These relationships will enable application service providers to access the transport networks that will carry their traffic. For example, consider the following:

- Relationships between transport providers (e.g., MCI WorldCom) and content providers (e.g., www.cnn.com and www.yahoo.com).

- Relationships between transport providers and caching providers (e.g., Akamai).

---

29    See discussion of traffic exchanges in section 3.4.2.1.

30    M. Kende, "The Digital Handshake: Connecting Internet Backbones" (OPP Working Paper No. 32, Federal Communications Commission, September 2000).

- Relationships between transport providers and electronic mail and Web-hosting service providers.

- Relationships between transport providers and new application providers.

It is important to recognize that new applications can quickly enter this space and radically change the landscape. Napster is an example of such an application. In less than a year, Napster raised a number of legal, policy, and architectural issues. It is this dynamic nature of the Internet that requires the government to use prudence when considering policy that impacts the Internet.

## 4.3 (Relationship C) Application Service Provider to Application Service Provider

The market segment for end-user applications services is characterized by low economies of scale. This is one factor that will keep this market sector competitive. Intermediate applications, however—such as those that facilitate end-user applications (e.g., telephony signaling, directory services, caching)—may become important from a public policy perspective if a single provider dominates and has the power to thrive without interconnection to other application service providers.

## 4.4 (Relationship D) Internet to Telecommunications Service Provider

For the foreseeable future, the emerging IP infrastructure needs to interconnect with selected parts of the legacy PSTN infrastructure.

# 5

# APPLICATION OF FRAMEWORK

In this chapter, we will apply the policy framework to several architectural issues that make IP unique.

### Table 5.1 Mapping of Architectural Issues to Framework Relationships

| IP Architectural Issues | Key Relationships |
|---|---|
| Service Levels | • IP Transport Provider to IP Transport Provider |
| | • IP Transport Provider to Application Service Provider |
| Routing | • IP Transport Provider to IP Transport Provider |
| | • IP Transport Provider to Application Service Provider |
| Multicasting | • IP Transport Provider to IP Transport Provider |
| Signaling | • IP Transport Provider to Application Service Provider |
| | • Application Service Provider to Application Service Provider |
| | • Internet to Telecommunications Service Provider |
| Caching | • Application Service Provider to Application Service Provider |

The analysis of each issue starts with a brief tutorial of the relevant technologies.

## 5.1  *Differentiated Levels of Service and QoS*

All networks provide some given quality of service. With POTS, quality of service is measured in terms of call-blocking probabilities, perceived quality of connection, and so on. With IP networks, a best-effort quality of service is the default level of service. "Best effort" implies that the medium is shared among all users, with no particular prioritization or guarantee of service. Applications such as e-mail, file transfers, and Web browsing can tolerate delays and variability of service.

A QoS network implies that a differentiated or guaranteed level of service is available. Services may be differentiated from one another by characteristics such as (1) maximum latency (amount of time that the message takes to go from sender to receiver), (2) maximum jitter (variation in latency), (3) minimum bandwidth (Kbps, Mbps, Gbps, or Tbps), (4) maximum packet loss (e.g., percent of packets dropped), and (5) minimum availability (percent of time that the service is available). Applications (such as telephony and video) that cannot tolerate the delays and variability of service above certain thresholds require these differentiated services with guaranteed performance.

Commercial deployments of QoS began to emerge (in the late 1990s) in the form of single-provider (intradomain) service offerings.[31] Even so, there are still fundamental issues that are not yet fully understood by experts developing these technologies. The Internet2 Qbone Working Group, a consortium focusing on research and development of QoS technologies, identifies three fundamental issues that affect the deployment of interdomain QoS:[32]

---

31    Global One (joint venture of Sprint Corp., Deutsche Telekom, and France Telecom) rolled out its Global Intranet VPN service with three classes of QoS in October 1999. Concert (joint venture of AT&T and BT) is scheduled to offer its Managed IP service with two levels of QoS January 2000. See http://www.teledotcom.com/422/sections/tdc422service_qos.html.

32    These issues are raised by Ben Teitelbaum of the Internet2 QBone Working Group. The Internet2 QBone is an interdomain testbed infrastructure built to support QoS research and experimentation. QBone is built on top of the Abilene and vBNS network backbones. The initiative seeks to facilitate the deployment of both intradomain and interdomain QoS technologies. The Internet2 QOS Working Group (comprised of both industry and university representatives) is primarily focusing on the three identified problems. Source: B. Teitelbaum, "Internet2 QBone: Building a Testbed for IP Differentiated Services" (INET99, San Jose, California, June 23, 1999).

- *Difficulty in understanding application requirements.* While some applications may require absolute, per-flow QoS assurances, others may be more adaptive and permit a minimum level of QoS that can be enhanced if additional network resources are available. There is also a perceived need for multiple classes of best-effort services with relative precedence levels. VoIP and interactive video have very stringent latency and jitter requirements. Streaming video has somewhat less stringent requirements, since the stream can be buffered to some extent. Data transfer applications, such as electronic mail or peer-to-peer file transfers, have less stringent requirements.

- *Problem of scalability.* The need to support QoS end-to-end, but to keep the per-flow state and packet-forwarding overhead out of the core networks.

- *Interoperability* between separately administered and designed clouds, and interoperability between multiple implementations of network elements.

There are a number of alternative architectural models for QoS in IP networks, including, but not likely limited to, the following: (1) overprovisioning (over-engineer capacity so that each application has ample bandwidth), (2) DiffServ (current focus of the Internet2 QBone initiative), (3) label switching (e.g., Multi Packet Label Switching [MPLS], ATM, and FR virtual circuits), (4) service marking (e.g., Internet Protocol version 4 [IPv4] Type of Service [ToS]), (5) relative priority marking (e.g., IPv4 precedence marking), (6) IntServ/ReSerVation Protocol (RSVP), and (7) static per-hop classification (variant of IntServ based on administrative time scales rather than particular flows).[33]

The Internet Engineering Task Force (IETF) standards process is currently focusing on the DiffServ and MPLS architectures for commercially viable QoS in an interdomain context. While each architectural model is somewhat different, there is a set of common underlying mechanisms that need to be implemented in each model. It is important for policy makers to have at least a superficial understanding of these QoS concepts (if not specific characteristics of particular implementa-

---

33    S. Blake, D. Black, M. Carlson, E. Davies, Z. Wang, and W. Weiss, "An Architecture for Differentiated Services" (IETF Informational RFC 2475, December 1998).

tions) to develop insight into appropriate and inappropriate public policies.[34] A list of important QoS concepts for policy makers is presented in Table 5.2 and then described in the paragraphs that follow.

### Table 5.2 Important QoS Concepts for Policy Makers

Admission control

Signaling protocols

Packet marking

Packet classification

Traffic shaping and conditioning

Priority mechanisms

Scheduling mechanisms

Queuing and congestion control algorithms

Policies and mappings between users, applications, and services

Bandwidth broker

Measurement tools

*Admission control* refers to the decision of whether a given connection or packet flow is permitted to enter the network. Decision criteria are based on fundamental issues, such as whether sufficient capacity is available to satisfy the request, and also on service provider preferences based on user identity, application identity, security requirements, and time-of-day/week. Once a connection has in principle been admitted to a network, there is an ongoing set of activities associated with the flow of packets that continue for the duration of the connection. These activities include packet marking, packet classification, traffic shaping/conditioning, priority/scheduling mechanisms, and queuing/congestion control mechanisms.

*Signaling protocols* are used by end-systems to request a desired level of QoS and also, possibly, to describe the traffic profile for which it will be used. Examples include the Resource RSVP, used in DiffServ and IntServ, and the Label Distribution Protocol (LDP) used by MPLS to ensure that adjacent routers have a

---

34    The discussion of QoS concepts borrows heavily from the IETF standards process, the Internet2 QBone Working Group, and the FAQ provided by the Quality of Service Forum.

common interpretation of labels. It is important to note that these signaling protocols are completely separate and different from telephony signaling protocols. QoS signaling supports a data delivery service, whereas telephony signaling supports an application service.

*Packet marking* refers to the setting of a particular value (or values) in a packet header to identify this packet as eligible for a given QoS treatment. In DiffServ, this value specifies the per-hop behavior (PHB) to be allocated to the packet within the provider's network. The packet marking is implemented by setting a DiffServ field value. In IPv4, the DiffServ field is the ToS octet; in Internet Protocol version 6 (IPv6) it is the traffic class octet.

*Packet classification* categorizes packets based on the packet's QoS markings. In DiffServ, this classification is used by routers to determine the appropriate forwarding behavior (which physically maps the packets into different queues that might get different treatment). MPLS uses labels to classify and map packets into a particular flow path. MPLS can be used to provide a transit service to DiffServ traffic by mapping the DiffServ field to an explicit path through an MPLS network.

*Traffic shaping and conditioning* ensures that the traffic entering a network adheres to a traffic profile specified in a Traffic Conditioning Agreement (TCA). The shaping/conditioning is performed by an ingress router. In DiffServ, the traffic conditioning function performs metering, marking, policing, and shaping. Metering compares the traffic pattern of each flow against the traffic profile. The QBone initiative is developing a QBone Measurement Architecture that will be able to answer questions such as "Is the expedited forwarding PHB working as expected?" Policing at the ingress edge routers aggregates the incoming traffic and compares it to the TCA. Shaping controls the forwarding rate of packets to (1) ensure compliance with the TCA, (2) ensure fairness between flows that map to the same class of service, and (3) avoid congestion.

*Priority mechanisms* ensure that higher-priority packets are served before lower-priority packets.

*Scheduling mechanisms* ensure that different flows (or connections) obtain their promised share of resources. They also ensure that spare capacity is distributed in a fair manner.

*Queuing and congestion control algorithms* are used by routers to decide in what order packets are to be forwarded. They also determine which packets are dropped when congestion occurs.

*Policies and mappings between users, applications, and services* are stored in a vendor-independent information model and schema (database design) that was developed by the Directory-Enabled Network (DEN) initiative. The model and schema will enable vendors to provide interoperable network services. For example, when a subscriber of an ISP asks for a service, that service must be delivered in an end-to-end fashion, possibly across multiple providers' networks. The model and schema specifications will enable vendors to have common service definitions, yet implement value-added services on top of these common elements. The DEN specification has been merged with the Common Information Model, which serves as the core information model for all IETF policy work.

A *bandwidth broker* is an agent and repository of policy priorities and limits for user and group access to bandwidth. The repository includes user credentials so that requests can be authenticated. The Bandwidth Broker (BB) is a part of the network infrastructure that has trusted, secure associations with all routers. Requests go from user to BB (so the BB can record use and resolve conflicts) and then to the appropriate router. This request path helps ensure that security is maintained. BBs keep track of the current allocation of marked traffic and interpret new requests in light of the policies and current allocation. An inter-BB signaling protocol is also under development to enable BBs to set up and maintain bilateral service agreements to accommodate interdomain (or provider-to-provider) QoS.

*Measurement tools* enable network operators to debug and audit QoS services that are being defined and developed (e.g., the QBone Measurement Architecture by the Internet2 QBone initiative).

## 5.1.1 (Relationship A) IP Transport Provider to IP Transport Provider

Current commercial deployments of QoS are just beginning to emerge in the form of single-provider (intradomain) service offerings.[35] Interdomain offerings look promising but are still in the research and development phase. From a public policy perspective, interconnection between competing IP transport service providers raises a number of issues to be understood and monitored.

---

35     Global One (joint venture of Sprint Corp., Deutsche Telekom, and France Telecom) rolled out its Global Intranet Virtual Private Network (VPN) service with three classes of QoS in October 1999. Concert (joint venture of AT&T and BT) is scheduled to offer its Managed IP service with two levels of QoS January 2000. See http://www. teledotcom.com/422/sections/tdc422service_qos.html.

First, it is important that one provider's BB be interoperable with another provider's BB to ensure that end-to-end QoS reservations can be made across provider boundaries. BBs will negotiate and/or implement SLAs that define the specific services to be delivered in a hierarchical or peer-to-peer relationship. Attributes of this agreement may include network service (e.g., bandwidth, latency), costs, measurement methods, and traffic conditioning rules. An SLA is implemented by service level specifications (SLSs) and/or Service Level Objectives (SLOs). A TCA specifies all traffic conditioning rules.

A second relationship issue is that of interoperable policy frameworks and schemas to ensure that policies are interpreted consistently and can be applied across domains.[36] Once these systems are interoperable, the service information stored within must be interpreted consistently as well. For example, if provider A uses a specific schema for describing the required bandwidth, latency, and jitter for a VoIP call, then the service information contained within this schema must be properly interpreted by provider B to ensure that this VoIP service is given the appropriate handling as the call traverses provider B's network.

A third relationship issue is that of ensuring that network operators have the means to do end-to-end debugging and auditing of QoS flows across multiple providers' networks. This requires both standards and authorization.

The financial settlements associated with guaranteeing a QoS service across multiple networks will likely be more complex than those associated with present-day peering (bill-and-keep) and transit (bill) arrangements. Guaranteed services entail both reservations and actual usage. The deployment of provider-to-provider QoS will depend on satisfactory settlement arrangements. Without a settlement process, the carriers may be encouraged to dump traffic onto other networks. To date, the technologies to support these settlements are not mature.

---

36    "One way to think of a policy-controlled network is to first model the network as a state machine and then use policy to control which state a policy-controlled device should be in or is allowed to be in at any given time. Given this approach, policy is applied using a set of policy rules. Each policy rule consists of a set of conditions and a set of actions. Policy rules may be aggregated into policy groups. These groups may be nested, to represent a hierarchy of policies." B. Moore, E. Elleson, and J. Strassner, "Policy Framework Core Information Model" (IETF Internet Draft, last accessed: October 1999).

## 5.1.2   (Relationship B) IP Transport Provider to Application Service Provider

These relationships will enable application service providers to offer bundled services (with guaranteed performance) to end users and resellers of services. For example, an IP telephony service provider may contract with an IP transport provider for a certain guarantee service or for several tiers of service. The IP telephony service provider could then, in turn, offer customers varying levels of service, each with a different price reflecting the underlying cost of the associated QoS transport. From a public policy perspective, the following elements of interconnection are important:

- Ability of application service providers to communicate with IP transport provider BBs to request services

- Ability of application service providers to interoperate with policy frameworks and schemas to ensure that these policies are interpreted consistently

- Ability of application service providers to interoperate with information repositories, such as DEN, to ensure consistent interpretation of service types and availability

- Ability for application service providers to measure end-to-end performance of QoS service

- Ability to support financial settlements

One might argue that there is no need for telecommunications policy here, since IP transport providers have incentives to ensure interoperability for their customers. However, there might be a need for policy to prevent a dominant IP transport provider offering application services from restricting competing providers' access to the transport.

## 5.1.3   (Relationship C) Application Service Provider to Application Service Provider

QoS is not an issue for the application-service-provider-to-application-service-provider relationship. QoS is a characteristic of an IP transport service. Application service providers interact with QoS in their relationships with IP transport providers.

### 5.1.4 (Relationship D) Internet to Telecommunications Service Provider

This relationship is not considered in this work.

## 5.2 Routing

To understand routing, it is useful to think of the Internet as a large number of interconnected networks. These networks must know how to reach one another in a dynamic manner as conditions change in the network. Routing is the coordinated process of determining the paths to the various destinations in the network. Routing protocols provide the router with the necessary information to move packets around the network efficiently. This process of orchestrating routes could be done through manually configuring routes in IP routing tables; however, this would be a laborious and ineffective process in such a large and dynamic environment. Therefore, routing protocols automate this process through a series of calculations that determine the best routes through the network. This information is stored in tables for use by routing protocols, such as IP, that actually perform the routing of the individual packets/datagrams.

The Internet is composed of interconnected local area networks (LANs) and wide area networks (WANs). It is useful to think of these segments as being broken down into autonomous systems. An Autonomous System (AS) is composed of routers and hosts logically belonging to one administrative group or organization. Figure 5.1 provides an example of several ASs combined into an Internet.

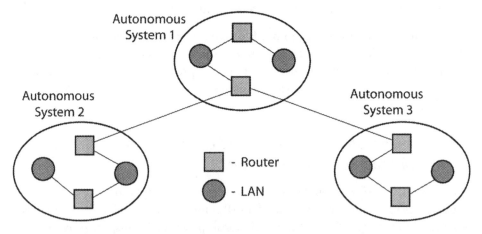

**Figure 5.1 Autonomous Systems (squares represent routers and circles represent LANs)**

Within each AS, routers make use of interior gateway protocols to share information on changes within the network—e.g., Routing Information Protocol (RIP),[37] Open Shortest Path First (OSPF),[38] and Interior Gateway Routing Protocol (IGRP).[39] Routers make use of exterior gateway protocols to share information between autonomous systems—e.g., Border Gateway Protocol (BGP)[40] and Exterior Gateway Protocol (EGP).[41] We briefly describe each of these protocols in the paragraphs that follow.

*Routing Information Protocol (RIP)* makes use of distance-vector routing protocols to calculate routes. The optimal route is determined by the shortest route to the desired destination. This distance is usually measured as the number of "hops" through the network. RIP allows routers in the same AS to periodically share routing updates through RIP updates. A router will both transmit updates and listen for updates from neighboring routers. These routers then use this information to update their own routing tables.[42, 43]

*Open Shortest Path First (OSPF)* provides routing information for large networks. Unlike RIP, which uses distance-vector algorithms, OSPF employs a link-state algorithm to determine best routes. Routers first synchronize their topological databases. After routers are synchronized, they update their routing tables. When a topological change occurs, the routers flood the network with topology information—a least-cost path is based on delay metrics, not hops. OSPF allows the administrator to preset preferred paths that override delay-based determinations. While OSPF is considered to be a far more complex algorithm, it is also far more powerful.

---

37  C. Hedrick, "RFC 1058—Routing Information Protocol" (IETF of the Internet Society, June 1988).

38  J. Moy, "RFC 2328—OSPF Version 2" (IETF of the Internet Society, April 1998).

39  Developed by Cisco Systems, Inc.

40  Y. Rekhter, "RFC 1771—A Border Gateway Protocol 4 (BGP-4)" (IETF of the Internet Society, March 1995).

41  D. L. Mills, "RFC 904—Exterior Gateway Protocol Formal Specification" (IETF of the Internet Society, April 1984).

42  RIP-2 (defined in RFC 1723) has improved on some shortcomings of RIP.

43  IGRP also overcomes operational problems of RIP. For more on IGRP, refer to RFCs 1131 and 1247.

In terms of interconnectivity, these interior protocols allow a network to optimize local connectivity by ensuring the best path through the network. A network administrator for a given AS has strong incentives to employ such protocols, so these protocols raise little concern for interconnection policies.

*Exterior Gateway Protocol (EGP and EGP-2)* is a routing protocol used to share network information between autonomous systems. More specifically, this protocol allows routers in different ASs to share reach information. Therefore, while RIP and OSPF provide routing information within ASs, EGP (and other exterior gateway protocols) allows routers existing on different ASs to share network reach information. At the edge of a network, a router will establish a trusted relationship with another network running EGP. This router will use the information obtained to create tables on the neighboring gateways, the networks to which these gateways are attached, and the distances associated with these possible routes.

*Border Gateway Protocol (BGP)*[44] is another exterior gateway protocol used to share reach information between networks. A BGP router establishes a relationship with another network's BGP router. A BGP router makes use of a "BGP speaker" to transmit and receive routing information over reliable connections. Transmission Control Protocol (TCP) connections are used to provide this reliable transport mechanism, making the periodic updates associated with EGP unnecessary. "Path attributes," contained in updates, provide information on routes to destination networks. Should more than one path exist, the BGP router determines the best path. BGP-4 is the most commonly used exterior gateway protocol.

The interconnection point at which IP traffic flows from one provider's network to another is called a traffic exchange point. NAPs (e.g., Metropolitan Area Exchange-West [MAE-West]) are an example of public, multilateral traffic exchange points. When two providers interconnect directly via one of their premises, this is called a private, bilateral traffic exchange point. There has been a great deal written in this area, including an FCC OPP Working Paper,[45] and so rather than attempt to add to that body of knowledge, we simply apply the framework as follows.

---

44    BGP includes a number of versions, including BGP 2, 3, and 4. BGP 4 is a commonly supported routing protocol.

45    M. Kende, "The Digital Handshake: Connecting Internet Backbones" (OPP Working Paper No. 32, Federal Communications Commission, September 2000).

## 5.2.1   (Relationship A) IP Transport Provider to IP Transport Provider

While interior gateway protocols are maintained within an AS, exterior gateway protocols require trust and cooperation between autonomous networks. This trust and cooperation has interconnection implications for IP transport providers. IP routing policies and filters provide a level of control for the exchange of routing information.[46]

*IP accept policies* control the additions of new routes to a routing table. When a routing protocol (interior or exterior) receives an update, it applies accept policies to determine whether the route should be added to the table. *IP announce policies* control the propagation of routing information through the network. Prior to route advertisement, a routing protocol will determine whether a route should be advertised by consulting announcement policies. These policies match a network to a specific action, and they provide the tools needed to promote cooperation and trust. The IETF is actively involved in developing the standards to support these policies and appears to be the logical place for such development.

The agreement to exchange routing information with another provider is generally part of a peering relationship. These relationships take the form of SLAs that define the relationship. Aside from merger conditions, the FCC has had little involvement in this area and does not appear to be moving into a more active role. Providers have long cooperated in the exchange of routing information, indicating that this process would not likely require involvement of the FCC. While this is true in today's best-effort Internet, the question arises as to whether the differentiation of services, the support needed for those services, and the potential profits obtained from those services might result in an unwillingness to exchange route information.

On a separate vein, the issues of security and reliability may distort the rather open process that is now in place. This may lead to national policies addressing these issues, but it is not clear who should develop such policies, particularly as they relate to national security. Following with the former chairman Kennard's "do no harm" policy, it would be advisable that the FCC continue to monitor this area.

---

46    IP import and export filters provide a similar function to IP accept and announce policies, but they are being discontinued.

### 5.2.2    (Relationship B) IP Transport Provider to Application Service Provider

With best-effort service networks, application service providers are typically transit customers of IP transport providers. America Online is an example, though, of an application service provider with sufficient market power to negotiate a peering arrangement with an IP transport provider.

With the emergence of interdomain QoS, SLAs will be used to implement the relationships between transport and application providers. These SLAs will identify service characteristics in terms more specific than the routing agreements that typify current peering and transit arrangements.

### 5.2.3    (Relationship C) Application Service Provider to Application Service Provider

Routing is not an application service provider issue, so routing between ASPs is irrelevant to this discussion.

### 5.2.4    (Relationship D) Internet to Telecommunications Service Provider

This relationship is not important to IP routing.

## 5.3    Multicasting

Currently, the predominant mode of transmission over the Internet is unicast. In other words, applications such as e-mail, file transfers, and browsers all utilize one-to-one communication. The next generation of applications running over the Internet, however, will employ a much wider range of communication formats, such as one-to-many, many-to-many, and many-to-one communication.

IP multicast is one of the primary packet types supported by IPv6, also referred to as IP next generation (IPng). As a technology, IP multicast simply provides an addressing mechanism for sending information from a single sender to multiple receivers. In practice, however, multicast can also be used to provide many-to-many and many-to-one communication. Examples of applications falling into each of the three categories are summarized in Table 5.3.[47]

---

47    https://datatracker.ietf.org/public/idindex.cgi?command=id_detail&id=4058.

## Table 5.3 Multicast Applications

| One to Many | Many to Many | Many to One |
|---|---|---|
| Scheduled audio/video | Multimedia conferencing | Resource discovery |
| Push media | Synchronized resources | Data collection |
| Caching | Concurrent processing | Auctions |
| Monitoring | Collaboration | Polling |
| Announcements | Distance learning | |
| | Chat groups | |
| | Interactive simulations | |
| | Multiplayer games | |

IP multicast is oftentimes associated solely with one-to-many communication in the delivery of multimedia. This characterizes only the first application listed in Table 5.3, scheduled audio/video, but IP multicast can be used for much more than multimedia delivery. In the basic one-to-many multicast model, one of the more promising applications of IP multicast is its facilitation in caching. As the number of online users continues to grow, so will the need for caching technologies and an efficient delivery mechanism for cached information.

Beyond one-to-many communication, IP multicast can also be used in many-to-many communication. In this situation, each node belongs to the multicast group and functions as both a sender and a receiver, with no notion of a hierarchy. Here, the primary goal is to efficiently distribute shared information across the network. As is evident from Table 5.3, "the many-to-many capabilities of IP multicast enable [some of] the most unique and powerful applications."[48]

Many-to-one communication is distinct from one-to-many and many-to-many communication by the fact that it utilizes both unicast and multicast. For example, in a resource discovery application, a node sends a multicast request. The node then receives a series of unicast responses. The end result, however, is another form of communication that is enabled by IP multicast.

Without support for multicast, communication for these types of applications can only occur via broadcast or replicated unicast transmissions. If at all possible,

48   Ibid.

broadcast and replicated unicast should be avoided due to the unnecessary duplication of information, which results in additional traffic and congestion. Under the unicast model of communication, the sender must maintain a list containing the IP address of each receiver. The sender then cycles through the list and sends information to each receiver independently. Figure 5.2 depicts a situation where there is a single sender and three receivers. The links with multiple lines indicate duplication of information and the points where IP multicast more efficiently manages bandwidth by reducing duplication.

**Figure 5.2 Unicast Model**

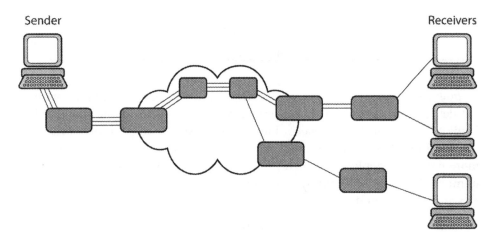

Under the multicast model of communication, the sender simply needs to be aware of the single group address to which all of the receivers are associated. Figure 5.3 depicts the same situation as Figure 5.2, but in this case, multicast is enabled across the network. The important distinction to be noticed is that the duplication of information across the network has been eliminated.

## Figure 5.3 Multicast Model

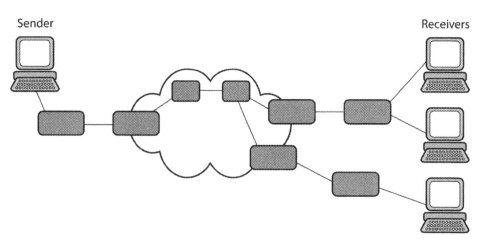

As one-to-many, many-to-one, and many-to-many applications become more popular, the need for multicast will increase. Without multicast to address the problem of duplication, the ability of the Internet to scale is in serious question. The current delivery method of scheduled audio/video applications, such as www. spinner.com and www.broadcast.com, provides a perfect example of scalability concern. In their current incarnation, these streamed services utilize replicated unicast. With each new user comes the need for yet another duplicate data stream taking up more and more bandwidth. Given the dramatic growth in the number of online users and the corresponding increase in streamed service use, the need for IP multicast becomes evident.

There are at least five distinct methods for routing multicasts. These approaches to multicast routing can be divided into two categories. The first category, "dense-mode" multicast routing, assumes that group members are densely distributed throughout the network. The second category, "sparse-mode" multicast routing, assumes that group members are sparsely distributed throughout the network. The main difference between the two categories is the amount of overhead required to maintain multicast routing tables. Dense-mode multicast routing generally requires much more bandwidth than sparse-mode multicast routing. Following is a list of the multicast routing protocols falling under each category.

### Table 5.4 Multicast Routing Protocols

| Dense-Mode Routing | Sparse-Mode Routing |
| --- | --- |
| Protocol-Independent Multicast—Dense Mode (PIM-DM) | Protocol-Independent Multicast—Sparse Mode (PIM-SM) |
| Multicast Open Shortest Path First (MOSPF) | Core-Based Trees (CBT) |
| Distance Vector Multicast Routing Protocol (DVMRP) | |

Multicasting fundamentally relies upon the notion of group membership. Applications, hosts, or users must have a method to both join and leave groups. Internet Group Message Protocol (IGMP) provides this functionality for IP multicast. Conceptually, IGMP parallels and operates at the same level as the Internet Control Message Protocol (ICMP). Both protocols act as a control mechanism between the host and an Internet gateway. Where ICMP's primary function is to report errors, IGMP's primary function is to report group membership.

The policy implications of multicast technologies, and their current state of deployment, are discussed along the lines of the interconnection relationships in sections 5.3.1 to 5.3.4.

### 5.3.1  (Relationship A) IP Transport Provider to IP Transport Provider

In order for multicast to become commercially viable, the entire network infrastructure must support multicast. Unfortunately, reaching a consensus on the multicast routing protocol that will be used has been a major roadblock. This has serious adverse policy implications for transport-to-transport relationships, since without an agreement on standards, interconnection of transport-to-provider multicast services will not be possible.

Multicast can be implemented across the full infrastructure by adopting a common multicast routing standard, or it can be supported by a subset of nodes via encapsulation. The positive side of using encapsulation is that not all intermediate routers need to support the same routing protocol or multicast. Such is the case with the experimental Multicast Backbone (MBONE) network, which uses DVMRP. MBONE encapsulates multicasts within ordinary IP datagrams and routes these packets across segments of the network that do not support MBONE multicasting.

The downside of relying on encapsulation and decapsulation (also referred to as tunneling) is that it entails a substantial overhead and can result in significant performance degradation. Consequently, unless each network hop is going to support more than one multicasting routing protocol, a full commercial deployment of IP multicast requires all routers to support the same routing protocol.

## 5.3.2   (Relationship B) IP Transport Provider to Application Service Provider

With IGMP becoming an Internet standard and the de facto means for membership reporting, the technology is in place for sufficient interconnection of application providers and transport providers.

Even if the network infrastructure has the necessary elements in place to support multicast, this does not mean that upper-layer protocols and/or applications will be able to take advantage of multicast. Multicast functionality has to be made available to the upper layers in order make the service useful. The latest version of IGMP, IGMP version 3 (IGMPv3), specifies "an Application Programming Interface or API used by upper-layer protocols or application[s] ... in order to take full advantage of the capabilities of IGMPv3."[49] Upper-layer protocols relying upon access to multicast functionality include Reliable Multicast Protocol (RMP) and Multicast File Transfer Protocol (MFTP). Currently, IP multicasts ride over the User Datagram Protocol (UDP), which is a best-effort service. Both RMP and MFTP operate at the transport layer and augment native multicast with a reliability mechanism. In so doing, a new set of applications becomes possible.

## 5.3.3   (Relationship C) Application Service Provider to Application Service Provider

Multicasting fundamentally relies upon the notion of group membership. Thus, the relationships between application service providers are important to multicasting. It is not clear, however, whether this multicasting relationship will (or should) fall within the purview of the FCC and telecommunications policy.

---

49   See http://www.ietf.org/internet-drafts/draft-ietf-idmr-igmp-v3-01.txt.

### 5.3.4 (Relationship D) Internet to Telecommunications Service Provider

This relationship is not important to IP multicasting.

## 5.4 Signaling

Signaling comprises the exchange of information used to complete, alter, manage, and terminate a call.[50] Signaling in the PSTN has a carrier-centric design in which carriers provide call connection and control through SS7 and INs.[51] These signaling networks are generally viewed as the complicated, hidden side of the PSTN, completely transparent to the user. In contrast, the Internet has a non-carrier-centric design (a decentralized control model) in which signaling may migrate to the edge of the network, away from carrier control. Services may be independent of the carrier, whereby the Internet carrier may simply provide the transport of bits.[52] Furthermore, unlike voice service over the PSTN,[53] an Internet service may be independent of the underlying transport network, thereby allowing for rapid innovation. Consider, for example, the continual evolution of Web browsers and their associated applications, which are independent of the underlying IP network.

Industry is investing significant effort and capital in developing IP telephony-related signaling protocols. However, a substantial installed base of customers will remain on the PSTN. To address this schism, a hybrid IP/PSTN architecture is developing. This approach requires gateways to translate between dissimilar networks and involves the conversion of the voice and control (signaling) data

---

50   The definition of signaling has been broadened here to include functions traditionally viewed as part of the IN—i.e., database access, voice response, and voice recognition systems.

51   Intelligent Network is used generically here to represent Intelligent Networks (INs) and Advanced Intelligent Networks (AINs).

52   Although the term "service" generally applies to functionality within the PSTN (e.g., voice service), here it is used more broadly to include Internet "applications" (e.g., Internet telephony).

53   There is incentive for providers in the PSTN to use signaling to control the provision of services. By controlling the signaling, the provider may charge for services, such as telephony. However, in an environment where users control signaling, interconnection of a service may require little involvement of the carrier.

between the circuit-switched and packet-switched networks. Such an approach will allow Internet users to complete simple voice calls or to access services typically provided by the IN.

Numerous signaling protocols are under development in the IETF and the International Telecommunications Union (ITU). These protocols are not mutually exclusive; in fact, many protocols will likely work in combination to provide services. There are three signaling protocols emerging within IP telephony: Session Initiation Protocol (SIP), H.323, and Media Gateway Control Protocol (MGCP). These protocols differ significantly in terms of control, design, and functionality. For example, SIP[54] provides a decentralized signaling functionality by allowing software residing in the user's device to initiate the telephone service. In contrast, a protocol such as MGCP[55] manages network elements using carrier-controlled call agents.[56] This design allows MGCP to control service features and to interoperate with SIP and H.323. H.323 is part of an ITU protocol suite evolving to address a broad range of IP issues, including network interoperability.[57, 58]

SIP is a peer-to-peer signaling protocol that allows the creation, modification, and termination of associations among end systems residing on the Internet. SIP provides much of the same functionality that presently resides in the PSTN signaling network.[59] SIP provides many services traditionally available in the PSTN, such as

---

54   This work is an effort of the IETF. See http://www.ietf.cnri.reston.va.us/ids.by.wg/mmusic.html.

55   SGCP and IPDC are merging to create the MGCP. See http://sgcp.bellcore.com/draft-huitema-sgep-v1-1-00.txt.

56   A call agent is a software element that serves to maintain or manage a call through the control of a gateway.

57   H.323 defines a broad suite of network protocols and is not limited in scope to IP telephony. In fact, H.323 was not originally designed for Internet telephony; rather, it started as a LAN multimedia protocol. See http://www.databeam.com/h323/h323primer.html.

58   H.323 defines a "gatekeeper" function that acts to manage traffic between gateways and to perform call control signaling. Gatekeepers also perform translation of addresses, bandwidth control, admission control, and management.

59   SIP provides the signaling necessary to establish the "call." Protocols such as Real-Time Transfer Protocol (RTP), RSVP, and Real-Time Control Protocol (RTCP) are involved in carrying the actual voice data. See http://www.isi.edu/div7/rsvp and http://www.cs.columbia.edu/~hgs/rtp.

call forwarding and transfer. Whereas control is centralized within the SS7/IN in the PSTN, SIP creates an environment in which control functions are distributed to the endpoints, into the user's device or elsewhere in the network.[60] A user may choose to obtain control data or functions from SIP servers maintained by third-party providers. In this environment, the telephone company is the provider of the "bit pipe," a path through the network.

MGCP plays an interesting role in the development of IP telephony.[61] MGCP is actually a merger of two prominent signaling protocols—Simple Gateway Control Protocol (SGCP) by Bellcore (now Telcordia) and Internet Protocol Device Control (IPDC) by Level3.[62] MGCP serves a particular niche, that of dumb end-systems design. In this design, gateways serve as dumb devices, with limited functionality and low cost. MGCP enables control and management of gateways at the edge of a network through software elements referred to as *call agents* (or media gateway controllers). The focus of this protocol is on defining the interface between the call agent and the gateway. In this design, MGCP can manage services by controlling the gateways, while making use of SIP or H.323 (operating at the edge of the network) to provide the necessary user signaling. MGCP assumes that the clients request their services using the same tones used by today's telephones. This ensures backward compatibility with the PSTN but also limits the functionality of the client.

The development of SS7 to IP interconnection raises a number of security and reliability concerns. The possibility of opening the signaling network to Internet-based attacks, such as denial of service, will require the industry to closely examine the security and reliability issues that might arise. The FCC is presently examining these concerns under the auspices of the Network Reliability Council.

### 5.4.1  (Relationship A) IP Transport Provider to IP Transport Provider

This relationship is not important to IP telephony signaling; signaling is an intermediate application that uses an IP transport service.

---

60    SIP and H.323 do make use of servers in the network (e.g., H.323 gatekeepers or SIP servers)—so, arguably, not all of the control resides at the user device.

61    See http://www.Level3.com/company/nov1698.html.

62    For more on SGCP, see http://sgcp.bellcore.com/draft-huitema-sgcp-v1-1-00/six. For more on IPDC, see http://www.level3.com/media.

## 5.4.2   (Relationship B) IP Transport Provider to Application Service Provider

These relationships will enable application service providers to offer bundled services to end users and resellers of services. For example, an IP telephony service provider may contract with an IP transport provider for QoS services. The IP telephony service provider could then, in turn, offer customers varying levels of service, each with a different price that reflects the underlying cost of the associated QoS transport. Note that an IP transport provider with market power seeking to offer VoIP services might attempt to throttle bandwidth/jitter for third-party VoIP offerings.

## 5.4.3   (Relationship C) Application Service Provider to Application Service Provider

Initially, IP service providers connecting to users on the PSTN may have strong dependencies on the IN for various functions, such as number translation.[63] This integration could have a profound influence on the future of IN service creation and provision. Functionality might develop to resemble IN functions, where service functionality could reside wholly within the Internet. This could further facilitate competition by allowing IP-based, third-party provision of services.

The ability of IP signaling to support third-party service providers enables a significant departure from traditional signaling in the PSTN. There is presently a certification arrangement that carriers require of one another to interconnect signaling networks. Interestingly, the FCC does not get directly involved in the certification process; rather, it relies on the carriers to fulfill their interconnection obligations. Some competitors claim that this is an anticompetitive arrangement and slows the market entry of new carriers. It is possible that this present process will not translate to IP telephony signaling, especially when one considers the number of potential players occupying this space. Therefore, this arrangement may require modification or removal. The new signaling players might include third-party service providers, as well as end users. With this design, it does not make sense for the industry to require this process. In fact, it might be necessary for the FCC to disallow such a requirement.

---

63   Number translation would use directory services for mappings between telephone numbers and IP addresses (or domain names).

The same trust and cooperation issues that must be addressed for transport-to-application service providers will need to be addressed in this space. What differentiates this from the transport-to-application issue is the inability of application providers to tie transport to the application. While this presents an interesting issue, application service providers presently are outside the scope of the FCC. As more services migrate to the Internet, Congress may perceive the need for some regulatory authority in this space.

### 5.4.4 (Relationship D) Internet to Telecommunications Service Provider

The signaling arrangements of the future will require substantial interconnection agreements among the new (e.g., CLECs and Data Local Exchange Carriers [DLECs]) and old (e.g., ILECs and IXCs) providers. The newer, IP-based signaling providers are considered application service providers because signaling is considered an intermediate application that utilizes the IP transport data delivery service. The providers of the older IN signaling are considered telecommunications service providers by virtue of their historical development and current regulatory classification. The question is, will arrangements between emerging and legacy signaling providers occur without regulatory intervention?

After the standards bodies resolve the details of emerging protocols, the question becomes one of implementation. A concern is whether carriers will enter willingly into signaling interconnection agreements. Within the PSTN, a certification process is required of a carrier before another carrier will interconnect signaling networks. While it is possible that a similar arrangement will develop for interconnecting with IP networks, many view this model as closed and inefficient. Within the Internet, SLAs provide the substance for interconnecting networks. Present peering agreements might shed light on how these arrangements may develop. Such agreements appear to operate effectively and efficiently through market-driven mechanisms. Moreover, the government has had little involvement in these arrangements, and it does not appear that such involvement is necessary. As the technology develops, it seems reasonable that similar agreements will develop between providers. Should a provider fail to provide signaling required to effectively interconnect a user with a service, it reasons that the provider might lose that user—especially since no single provider will likely be able to control the entire market. Should a provider establish such a position, the threat of intervention by the Department of Justice (DoJ) should discourage a provider from exerting market dominance. Therefore, while it is in the FCC's best interest to ensure interconnectivity of emerging and legacy signaling systems, it also appears that it is in the provider's best interest to interconnect. It is interesting to note that some of the critical concerns that face the PSTN diminish in an IP telephony environment. The notion of an unbundled-signaling network element becomes unnecessary in an IP telephony environment. As long as providers can obtain the required level of service, it is possible to support a voice application.[64]

It is likely that nondisclosure obligations will be placed on many of the SLAs into which these companies enter, obviously making the details unknown outside this relationship. Nondisclosure has long been the practice for peering SLAs, and whether this is harmful to the industry is subject to debate. Recognizing that signaling is far more complex than packet exchange, it may be necessary for the industry to develop guidelines detailing interoperator signaling requirements.[65] Such requirements could then service as a guideline for private negotiations between providers. As was the case in the PSTN, the FCC should allow the industry to develop these documents.

## 5.5  Caching

As with IP multicast, caching[66] is another method for the efficient distribution of information to the edges of a network. Efficiency gains occur by temporarily storing copies of commonly accessed information in caches throughout the network. The goal of positioning caches close to the user is to reduce "response time, server load and network bandwidth consumption."[67] In practice, caching has been extremely successful and holds a tremendous amount of promise in helping the Internet to scale. Currently, there are two major forms of caching within the

---

64   User-controlled signaling does not mandate any special network arrangements. Carrier-controlled signaling, on the other hand, requires a number of interconnection agreements in order to maximize the full potential of the technology. As with IP multicast, these agreements can be described within the framework for interconnection.

65   These guidelines might be similar to signaling specifications maintained by Telcordia.

66   http://www.ietf.org/internet-drafts/draft-ietf-wrec-taxonomy-01.txt provides a taxonomy for caching that essentially follows the framework for interconnection. This section essentially takes the taxonomy and reapplies it to the framework.

67   Ibid.

Internet.[68] The first type of caching, *user agent caching,* is done at the endpoints themselves. By definition, a user agent cache is integrated within the application that utilizes the cache. The most common instance of this type of cache is the one that is maintained within Web browsers. Web browsers with caching not only display the results of browsing requests but also store the results of the most recent requests for subsequent retrieval. The obvious benefit of user agent caching is that duplicate requests can be loaded locally without having to go across the network again.

The second type of caching, *proxy caching,* is done at any point in the network between multiple clients and multiple servers. As the name suggests, proxy caching is done by a proxy. A proxy is simply an "intermediary system which acts as both a server and a client for the purpose of making requests on behalf of other clients."[69] Caching proxies can be organized into either a *cache cluster* or a *caching mesh.* A cache cluster logically operates as a single cache by providing the same service to all clients regardless of the caching proxy providing the actual service. A caching mesh is a "loosely coupled" set of proxies or clusters that share cacheable content but operate independently.[70] By overlaying a network of caching proxies on top of the network of servers and clients, tremendous gains in network performance can be made.

With the goal of developing a network of interdependent caches, a number of mechanisms for intercache and network element communication must be in place before such a goal is attainable. Intercache communication concerns the communication and coordination between caching proxies. Network element communication concerns the communication and coordination between caching proxies and network elements, such as routers and switches. Protocols and mechanisms involving intercache communication include Internet Cache Protocol (ICP), Hyper Text Caching Protocol (HTCP), Cache Array Routing Protocol (CARP), Cache Digest, and Cache-prefilling. Protocols and mechanisms involving network element communication include Web Cache Coordination Protocol (WCCP), Transparent Proxy Agent Control Protocol (TPACP), and SOCKS. As is obvious, there are a number of takes on intercache and network element communication. It is incumbent upon providers to be aware of the state of the art in caching to do their best to support its implementation.

---

68    http://www.w3.org/Conferences/WWW4/Papers/155/.

69    http://www.ietf.org/internet-drafts/draft-ietf-wrec-taxonomy-01.txt.

70    Ibid.

Although the actual cache resides at the caching proxy, clients still must be made aware of the proxy's location in order to use the caching proxy instead of the origin server. Currently, a number of methods exist for proxy discovery. The most rudimentary method for proxy discovery is via *manual proxy configuration.* Users simply manually configure their clients with the relevant proxy protocol information and location. This method, however, is error prone, cumbersome to users, and not very viable in a full commercial deployment of proxy caches. Thus, a number of more formal methods for client-to-proxy configuration have arisen. The primary methods are Proxy Auto Configuration (PAC) and Web Proxy Auto-Discovery Protocol (WPAD). PAC is a JavaScript page that provides clients with pointers to caching proxies. The downside to this method is that users must again supply the location of the machine providing the PAC service. Enter WPAD. WPAD is a protocol whose primary function is to provide the location of a PAC service. WPAD is implemented via standard discovery protocols such as Domain Name Service (DNS), Service Location Protocol (SLP), and Dynamic Host Configuration Protocol (DHCP). The end result is a client capable of automatically connecting to the closest possible cached services. With supporters such as Inktomi, Microsoft, RealNetworks, and Sun Microsystems, WPAD promises to be a major defining force in the implementation of future caching services.

In terms of interconnection, user agent caching does not mandate any special arrangements. Caching proxies, on the other hand, require a number of interconnection agreements in order to maximize the full potential of caching as a technology. As with IP multicast, these agreements can be described within the framework for interconnection.

### 5.5.1 (Relationship A) IP Transport Provider to IP Transport Provider

This relationship is not important to IP caching. Caching is an intermediate application that uses an IP transport service.

### 5.5.2 (Relationship B) IP Transport Provider to Application Service Provider

Better network performance can be achieved through caching content "closer to the eyeballs," or by providing a higher-performance IP transport service. There are tradeoffs to be made here. The cost-effectiveness of these tradeoffs and the ability for third-party caching make the relationship between a caching provider (application service) and an IP transport provider potentially important to public policy.

### 5.5.3   (Relationship C) Application Service Provider to Application Service Provider

Caching is an application that uses an IP transport service.

In many respects, caching proxies could be thought of as a public repository of information. By allowing open access to and open exchange between these repositories, significant gains in network performance can be made. As with most of the technologies mentioned within this section, however, policy makers need to be aware that caching could be used in an anticompetitive manner. For example, providers have to give WPAD-enabled clients access to the standard discovery protocols previously described. Restricting access to these protocols is one form of restricting interconnection between application service providers.

### 5.5.4   (Relationship D) Internet to Telecommunications Service Provider

This relationship is not important to IP caching.

## 5.6   In Summary

There are a number of services/technologies that might be considered within the terms of this framework. For example, directory services, billing, and network management present additional interconnection policy differences worth considering. Rather than attempt to be comprehensive with this analysis of interconnection issues, we hope to provide insight and to motivate additional analyses of emerging interconnection issues.

The observations from this chapter provide inputs for policy direction discussed in chapter 6. While much of the analysis may indicate that regulatory intervention is not presently required, it is the examination process that affords some structure for analyzing this complex problem. The results of the analysis raise concerns, indicate the areas that the FCC should more closely observe, and also indicate the areas that industry should work together to resolve.

# 6

# POLICY IMPLICATIONS

Considering the analysis from chapter 5, the transport-to-transport and transport-to-application spaces raise interesting interconnection issues. Of particular interest is the control that could be exerted by companies that lead in either of these spaces. Companies that dominate both the transport and the application spaces may raise concerns. These providers have the greatest incentive and best position to exert such dominance. While this has always been the case for ISPs, the transition from best-effort to guaranteed services fundamentally changes the competitive landscape. The problem this raises for regulators centers on mergers in the industry. Companies recognize the business potential that exists by being a dominant player in the future Internet, and they are building infrastructures that can best leverage that potential. As the dominant players become larger and fewer, this concern becomes even greater.

At the transport-to-application level, many of the same tools described previously might apply. The important difference here is that access to applications is at the heart of what makes the Internet so valuable. The value of the Internet is that a user can access most any site that connects to the Internet. If application services, particularly intermediate services such as telephony signaling and caching, are incorporated into the network, such access may become more complex. This may also impact the ability of third-party application service providers to offer users services without being required to enter into business agreements with the underlying transport network provider. It may also limit the user's ability to access information. The transport-to-application relationship in our framework will likely be of most significance as the Internet develops into a real-time network. The applications will be the value of the network, and transport providers may have the incentive to keep users on their network, if only to maintain revenue streams. It appears to the authors that this is the crux of future interconnection policy.

The same issues that must be addressed for transport-to-application service providers will need to be addressed for application-to-application providers. What distinguishes this from the transport-to-application issue is the inability of application providers to tie transport to the application. While anticompetitive posturing may still occur, application service providers presently are outside of the FCC's regulatory jurisdiction. However, as services migrate to the Internet, many more issues will arise. How government addresses these issues may well determine how the Internet develops.

At the transport-to-transport level, a number of policy tools can be used to address the anticompetitive concerns that might arise. The first is to rely on the use of antitrust laws. Another option would be to rely on merger conditions in order to implement certain interconnection agreements. This, of course, has narrow scope (applying only to the merged company), but it may be effective considering the market share of mergers. Another option would be to make use of the FCC's authority under Section 256 of the 1996 Telecommunications Act. This section provides the FCC with broad authority to enter the standards process when it believes that such intervention is required, or it at least allows the FCC to threaten such actions. The next option would be for Congress to revise the Communications Act to account for the fundamentally different Internet environment that will soon exist. Major revisions that replace the media-specific approach with more general rules that adhere to layers (such as those proposed in this book) could incorporate a new series of interconnection obligations. One such rule might be along the lines of open interconnection for transport providers.

The Internet-to-telecommunications service relationship represents the interface between critical elements of the legacy PSTN (e.g., telephony signaling and directory services) and what are considered application services (intermediate applications) in an IP infrastructure—i.e., telephony signaling and directory services. These applications depend on the underlying facilities for transport.

As indicated in the chapter 5 analysis, much of the substance of interconnection boils down to competitive markets, effective SLAs, and open standards. This belief is premised on a market-based approach to telecommunications policy.

## 6.1   Mechanisms for Ensuring Interconnection

To promote interconnection, there will always be some need for coordination and cooperation. In a market-driven environment, standards and SLAs may replace much of the regulatory requirements presently placed on carriers. Interconnection between carriers requires both the *incentive* and the *ability* to interconnect. A carrier may not have the incentive to interconnect because of a dominant market position or because of a particular business strategy. However, assuming a carrier does have the incentive to interconnect still requires the ability. Standards and SLAs provide this ability. While recognizing that there may always be some regulatory component in the mix, this chapter briefly examines SLAs and standards mechanisms, and it explores how these mechanisms might promote interconnection.

### 6.1.1   SLAs

The creation and enforcement of SLAs will likely become a more important issue as we move away from a best-effort Internet. SLAs will take the form of more complex agreements with many facets. They will require more substance to address the great variety of protocols and services that a guaranteed-service (QoS) Internet will demand. In such an environment, there will likely be fewer regulatory obligations and, possibly, fewer tariffs. Carriers will need to rely heavily on these arrangements. There will likely be more competition (more players) and more services (voice, browsing, e-mail, and video), allowing for more reliance on the market and less reliance on regulation.

An SLA specifies the terms of agreement and, for a specific service (application or transport), it will describe performance guarantees, tracking methods, reporting methods, problem management, customer responsibilities, security, termination policies, and payment penalties. The nature of performance measurements will differ between application and transport services, but reporting methods and other policies may be similar.

### 6.1.2   Standards

The FCC recognizes that open standards groups represent the best place for standards efforts to take place. However, the FCC might consider a more active monitoring role with standards organizations. This might include relying more heavily on Federal Advisory Committee Act (FACA)[71] to provide guidance. The FCC may take on a more active role as an observer of the standards process, as

---

71    FACA, 5 U.S.C., App. (1988), applies to any advisory committee established or utilized by one or more agencies in the interest of obtaining advice or recommendations for federal agencies. The Act states that new advisory committees should be established only when they are determined to be essential. Specifically, FACA requires that these committees must have functions that cannot be performed by FCC staff or by an existing committee, must be in the public interest in connection with the performance of duties imposed on the FCC by law, must advise only (actual determinations must be made by the FCC), and must be terminated when they no longer carry out their designated purpose. An advisory committee created under FACA must have a membership fairly balanced in terms of the points of view represented. Under FACA, advisory committees are not considered to be in effect until a charter for the committee has been filed with Congress.

Additionally, under FACA, meetings must be open to the public, detailed meeting minutes must be prepared, and a designated federal official must be present at all meetings. General Services Administration (GSA) regulations implementing FACA set out specific requirements for publishing announcements that establish the committee and scheduled meetings, including meeting agendas, in the *Federal Register*. For example, announcements of a meeting and meeting agenda must be published at least fifteen days prior to the meeting, and only under exceptional circumstances may this period be shortened. Announcements of committee establishment must be published in the *Federal Register* at least fifteen days before the committee charter is filed with Congress, but a waiver for a shorter period is permissible.

Both FACA and the implementing GSA regulations also set out specific reporting requirements, both annual and periodic (transcripts, meeting minutes, and so on). Each advisory committee is responsible for keeping records, transcripts, minutes, appendixes, and working papers and for making them available for public inspection. Each advisory committee is also responsible for keeping detailed records of certain information that the agency's committee management officer (CMO) uses to prepare the agency's annual Advisory Committee Report and Management Plan. The required information includes, for example, the committee name; the date of and authority for creation of the committee; the committee's termination date or date it is to make a report; the committee's functions; reference to the reports the committee has submitted; a statement of whether the committee is an ad hoc or continuing body; the dates of committee meetings; names and occupations of current members; and the total estimated annual cost to the United States to fund, service, supply, and maintain the committee. The FCC's CMO will provide each advisory committee with a form to complete that will ask for information such as that listed above. In addition, each advisory committee is responsible for completing time and expense logs.

it has done with DSL standards and the T1E1.4 working group.[72] This includes encouraging participation by all segments of industry, as suggested in the Second Report and Order on Advanced Services.[73] Policy makers may require standards groups to demonstrate certain characteristics before relying on these groups to support development of technical policy. These characteristics might include open membership, equal participation, timeliness, nondominance, and possibly international orientation. The importance of timeliness cannot be understated. Whether deliberate or inadvertent, the slow progress of standards creates numerous problems, particularly as innovation increases its pace.

The IETF[74] is one example of a standards organization upon which the FCC may rely for standards. IETF standards processes are intended to ensure technical excellence, reflect completed implementation and testing, include clear and concise documentation, be based on open and fair proceedings, and be timely. These goals appear to represent a well-conceived approach for future standards processes.[75] It is worth mentioning that multiple standards have long been a problem in telecommunications, and this will likely continue to some extent. The FCC has generally not made decisions as to the winner when multiple standards compete.

## 6.1.3   Monitoring Interconnection

In both the near term and beyond, the FCC may monitor development of interconnection. This notion of observing the market before making any potentially damaging requirements aligns well with the former chairman Kennard's vision of

---

72   The FCC has taken an active role in monitoring spectrum management standards in T1E1.4. See, for example, "In the Matters of Deployment of Wireline Services Offering Advanced Telecommunications Capability and Implementation of the Local Competition Provisions of the Telecommunications Act of 1996," Third Report and Order in CC Docket [Common Carrier Docket] No. 98–147 and Fourth Report and Order in CC Docket No. 96–98, 14 FCC Rcd. 20,912, 14 FCC Rcd. 20,912 (December 9, 1999).

73   "In the Matter of Deployment of Wireline Services Offering Advanced Telecommunications Capability," First Report and Order and Further Notice of Proposed Rulemaking in CC Docket No. 98–147 (March 31, 1999).

74   http://www.ietf.org/overview.html.

75   This is only one of many possible approaches that might service well to create new standards.

"do no harm."[76] There are a number of things worth investigating, as outlined in table 6.1.

### Table 6.1 Potential Areas for FCC Monitoring

- Provision of new services
- Development of national and international standards
- Public satisfaction
- Backbone and ISP competition
- SLAs

Aside from collecting information, monitoring may also have the effect of inducing desired behavior. It is less likely for parties to stray into anticompetitive behavior if they know they are being monitored. The FCC is already monitoring the market, as in the 706 Notice of Inquiry (NOI),[77] watching for failures, and possibly exerting regulatory authority when this process fails.

---

76   William E. Kennard, "The Road Not Taken: Building a Broadband Future for America" (speech of then FCC Chairman William E. Kennard before the National Cable Television Association, Chicago, Illinois, June 15, 1999).

77   "In the Matter of Inquiry Concerning the Deployment of Advanced Telecommunications Capability to All Americans," Notice of Inquiry in CC Docket 98–148 (FCC-0057), released February 18, 2000.

# 7

# FINDINGS

In this book, we present a framework for considering future telecommunications policy for interconnection. We highlight the fundamental shift that will be required to understand and create sound regulatory policy for future networks in terms of interconnection. It is clear that prior policy on interconnection does not port well to future demands. It is also clear that as difficult as interconnection has been in POTS (and the early data world), in the IP environment this problem may become intractable by relying on present regulations. Considering this heightened complexity, along with the general shift toward a dependence on the marketplace, the FCC should be particularly cautious of applying previous common carriage interconnection obligations on new carriers. This is not to say that a new notion of common carriage obligation will not develop, only that the previous rules create contradictions and inconsistencies. Further, at this point in time, no one can accurately predict what policies might be required.

The following is a list of interconnection issues for the reader to consider. This is intended to highlight areas of concern and to indicate directions that might be considered. It is not intended to dictate future FCC policy on interconnection, nor is it a predictor of future policy directions.

### Table 7.1 Summary of Takeaway Interconnection Issues

| Nature of Policy Issue | Explanation |
|---|---|
| Interconnection occurring at multiple levels in the Internet | Interconnection exists at many more layers in the Internet than in the PSTN. |

| Nature of Policy Issue | Explanation |
| --- | --- |
| Fundamental differences in interconnection as we move toward IP networks | There are fundamental differences between an IP environment and the PSTN. Interconnection in the Internet differs with the PSTN from the perspective of industry, regulation, network architecture, bandwidth, signaling, and more. |
| Treatment of packet networks | Previous FCC obligations on packet networks (i.e., ATM or FR) have been vague and of little substance. The FCC should carefully define a future policy that ensures a balance of connectivity, investment, and innovation. This requires maintaining a separation between that which is regulated and that which is not. |
| Technological interpretation of interconnection of public packet-switched networks | Networks and services are changing as a result of technical innovation. The notion of interconnection will expand to include functions and services that are not part of the POTS experience. |
| Rate of technical change | It may be shortsighted to identify specific technologies or implementations of technologies in this document or in any functional requirement for interconnection. Both evolve at a rate far faster than that with which a regulatory body can or should keep up. |
| Distinction between IP transport and applications that use an IP transport service | *IP transport* is the term used to denote the IP data delivery service. From a policy and perhaps business perspective, this service is distinct from the application services that use the IP transport service. These application services may be intermediate application services (such as telephony signaling and caching), end-user application services (such as electronic mail or video streaming), or content services (such as news sites). |
| Transport-provider-to-transport-provider interconnection | The desire to maintain a highly interconnected network may ensure that carriers freely interconnect with one another, providing that this type of interconnection will require the development of standards together with the use of extensive service level agreements. However, should this fail, policy makers may need to become active in this area. Policy makers might require a company to make public its terms of interconnection (be it peering or transit) and allow other carriers to connect according to those terms. |

| Nature of Policy Issue | Explanation |
|---|---|
| Transport-provider-to-application-provider interconnection | This relationship is difficult to define within the PSTN. At one level, interconnection of the application (voice) to the transport (the PSTN) is a regulated obligation and so exists. However, when we consider the failure of third-party IN services, attempts to create such an environment within the PSTN have failed. This same type of failure may well be the biggest threat to the future Internet. Based on the analysis in chapter 5, there appear to be sufficient opportunities (and likely sufficient incentive) for transport providers to lock out competitive application providers. This is particularly the case as the Internet becomes a real-time network and carriers can demand higher prices for services such as voice or video. |
| Internet-to-telecommunications interconnection | This relationship reflects the interaction of the emerging infrastructure and legacy infrastructure. Policy makers should closely monitor this area, particularly signaling and directory services. |
| Monitoring | One of the roles that the FCC could provide is to monitor the development of interconnection. This notion of observing the market prior to making any potentially damaging requirements aligns well with the former chairman Kennard's vision of "do no harm." |
| Utilization of Enforcement Bureau | The recent restructuring of the FCC suggests that the Enforcement Bureau will play a more active and critical role in carrying out policy. In keeping with this direction, obligations should rely on Enforcement mechanisms that could levy fines or take other corrective action. This approach assumes that some level of regulation would exist and therefore may not apply well to a largely unregulated industry. |
| Impact of technology on the interconnection of public IP networks | As packet networks replace the circuit-switched world, interconnection may become a more powerful competitive tool, particularly when one considers QoS requirements such as the carriage of real-time traffic. Technology will likely continue to distort our notion of interconnection. The question that remains is how to create policy that ensures interconnection while not having a detrimental effect on innovation and investment. Such policy may require more general obligations divorced from the underlying technology. |

| Nature of Policy Issue | Explanation |
|---|---|
| A new space for Internet players | The possible direction of future interconnection policy will be to create a new regulatory space, one where players now occupying various Title spaces could migrate. The approach would be to create a small number of general requirements, as described in chapter 6, which would ensure the public interest while allowing the market to operate without excessive regulatory obligations. It may well be that the current information service distinction will serve in the near term. |
| Mergers | Mergers that are occurring between the providers of the *conduit* and the providers of the *content* may require closer scrutinizing. Many believe the promise of the Internet is to provide diverse access to an almost unbounded amount of information. This also means the ability to distribute information in a similarly open manner. Such access and distribution will become difficult, if not impossible, if those that control the network refuse to interconnect with content providers in a meaningful manner. This becomes a real concern as we move to content that requires transport of a certain QoS level. |

As the PSTN and the Internet converge, the present regulatory structures begin to lose meaning. The notion of what defines a cable service or what defines telephony service becomes a matter of debate. Government should be cautious about applying rules from the present regulatory model to the emerging Internet model. This caution should be applied to common carrier, radio, cable, and broadcast alike. If caution is not exercised, the result could be an unnecessarily regulated environment that would stifle investment and thereby stall the development of high-speed services. Further, the regulations of the past were designed to ensure universal access to an application—namely, voice—in a monopoly environment; in contrast, the basic element in the Internet is a bit-pipe, or data delivery, service that is independent of any particular application making use of the pipe or service.

The difficulties associated with translating the existing application-specific regulatory model to the emerging telecommunications infrastructure may seem to be a compelling argument for why the Internet should not be regulated. However, rather than claim that the Internet should not be regulated, we point out areas where policy makers need to keep close tabs. It is the opinion of the authors that the relationship between a distinct transport service provider and a distinct application provider is at the heart of the Internet. Again, the mergers that consolidate transport and application will most harm the competitive landscape, particularly in the future Internet.

A role for regulatory agencies will be to develop general policies that foster innovation and competition for high-speed services—a policy that might encourage an open service environment through reasonable interconnection and access measures reminiscent of the traditional Internet.

The authors welcome insight and comment from policy makers and from the public on all matters discussed in this book. Please direct e-mail to douglas.sicker@ colorado.edu, jmindel@sfsu.edu, or cooper_c@fortlewis.edu.

# 8

# AFTERWORD

The original draft of this book was prepared during the summer of 1999, yet the primary message is still relevant today. Interconnection issues associated with IP networks and applications are fundamentally different and more complex than that with which telecommunications legislation, regulation, and policy makers have previously had to grapple. The explanations and layered framework presented in this book are intended as a guide.

In deciding to publish this work in 2006, we grappled with the issue of how much and to what extent the original manuscript should be updated. We opted to maintain the tone of the original document and then provide selective updates in this afterword. Three sets of updates are presented:

- Refined layered model (described in chapter 4) that was published in 2002

- Very brief synopses of several publications that reference the 1999 unpublished manuscript

- Demonstration of how the layered model is relevant to several important telecommunications policy issues that emerged at the time of publication

## *Refined Layered Model*

The framework presented in chapter 5 was refined in a 2002 journal publication.[78] That refinement is described here. Readers wishing to quickly contrast the original and refinement are referred to Table 8.1, Table 8.2, Figure 8.1, Figure 8.2, and Figure 8.3.

To define the layers correctly, one must consider the services provided and the structure of the network. The framework should allow policy makers to systematically evaluate interconnection relationships between providers. The layers distinguish between types of physical services (e.g., access, transport), application services (e.g., directories, caching, electronic mail), content services, and legacy telecommunications services (i.e., traditional PSTN telephony). These categories are further described in Table 8.1.

### Table 8.1 Categories of Services Offered

| Service Category | Explanation |
| --- | --- |
| Physical services | Providers of (1) access services and (2) transport services; includes both best-effort and QoS services. These may include network operators, NAP operators, and GigaPOPs.[79] |
| Application services | Providers of application services that rely on underlying access and transport services can be further subdivided into three subcategories: (1) directory service providers (e.g., DNS), (2) intermediate or middle service providers (e.g., multicasting and caching), and (3) end-user service providers (e.g., electronic mail, Web hosting, search engines). One could argue that these three subcategories are distinct and should be treated as such, but this broad categorization is sufficient for this context. The point is to distinguish between the provision of a data delivery service and the entities that use the data delivery service. The specific interconnection differences that arise for each of these three subcategories are beyond the scope of this book. |

---

78   D. Sicker and J. Mindel, "Refinements of a Layered Model for Telecommunications Policy," *Journal of Telecommunications and High Technology Law* 1, no. 1 (2002): 69–94.

79   A GigaPOP, unlike a NAP, is a layer-three interconnection point that allows for aggregation of resources and access to services in a cost-effective manner.

| Service Category | Explanation |
|---|---|
| Content services | Content providers that rely on underlying transport, access, application-directory, and application-intermediate services. Examples of content include video, music, and telephony services. |
| Legacy telecommunications services | Telecommunications service providers as generally defined in the Communications Act. |

One could also argue that software developers and consumers are also crucial to the deployment and use of the infrastructure, and they should therefore be included in the framework. Software developers are not, however, generally subject to telecommunications policy today.[80] Services and service providers tend to be of concern, rather than those parties that actually develop the services on behalf of the service providers. Consumer benefits and costs are central motivating factors in telecommunications policy, but since they are not directly associated with the interconnection of provider networks, they are also beyond the scope of this interconnection analysis. This book refers to the heterogeneous group of providers that provide the emerging IP infrastructure (i.e., access providers, transport providers, application service providers, and content providers) as ISPs. As mentioned earlier, some view the separation of the IP service from the physical transport as a beneficial distinction; we do not make that distinction in this model.

This layered stack provides a framework for systematic evaluation of the interconnection relationships between the layers. From the perspective of interconnection policy, the most important provider relationships are those listed in Table 8.2 and depicted in Figure 8.1 and Figure 8.2.

**Table 8.2 Refined Layered Model Relationships**

| Short Name | Explanation |
|---|---|
| Relationship A | Access Provider to Access Provider |
| Relationship B | Access Provider to Transport Provider |

---

80   Although they are subject to Section 255 (Disability) of the Communications Act, 47 U.S.C. § 255 (Supp. V 1999) and the Communications Assistance to Law Enforcement Act ("CALEA"), 47 U.S.C. § 1002 (Supp. V 1999).

| Short Name | Explanation |
|---|---|
| Relationship C | Transport Provider to Transport Provider |
| Relationship D | Transport Provider to Application Service Provider |
| Relationship E | Application Service Provider to Application Service Provider |
| Relationship F | Application Service Provider to Content Service Provider |
| Relationship G | Internet Service Provider to Telecommunications Service Provider |

Relationships A through F are depicted in Figure 8.1 and Figure 8.2.

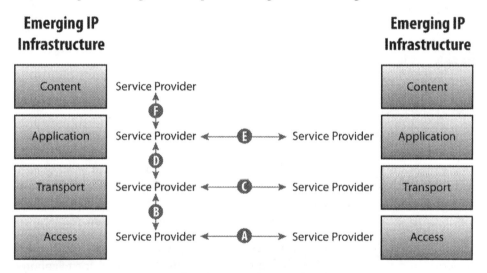

**Figure 8.1 Refined Layered Model Relationships**

Figure 8.1 shows a conceptual (simplified) protocol stack that providers of IP infrastructure might employ. From an interconnections policy perspective, these layers are of primary interest. For example, transport providers will use applications on their networks, but since they offer the transport service to the public for a fee, the transport is the service of interest. Similarly, caching providers will employ an Intranet to interconnect their caches and to connect their caches to the public transport network. Since they offer the caching service to the public for a fee, caching is of interest, not their private Intranets.

Figure 8.2 depicts Relationship G, between ISPs and telecommunications service providers. The diagonal layering implies that PSTN voice and PSTN transport services are more tightly coupled than are the modular layers in the emerging IP infrastructure.

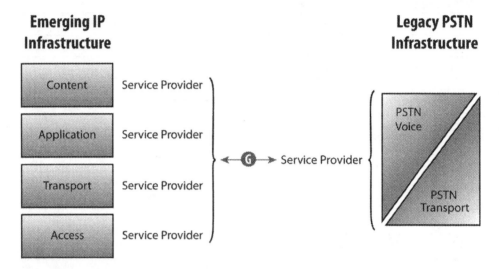

**Figure 8.2 Relationship Between IP and PSTN Infrastructure Providers**

In Figure 8.2, services that would be considered application services in an IP context (e.g., SS7/IN and directory services) are in the upper diagonal, and those services that would be considered transport services are in the lower diagonal. Both are considered *telecommunications services* in legacy PSTN regulation.

Figure 8.3 depicts an abstracted interconnection between the emerging IP infrastructure and the legacy PSTN infrastructure that might be used for telephony. The two linkages between the infrastructures reflect separate network connections for voice and signaling.

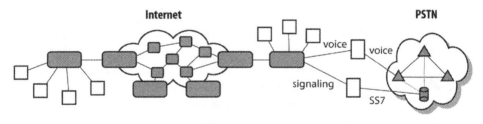

**Figure 8.3 Abstracted Telephony Interconnection Between Infrastructures**

The seven interconnection relationships (A through G) are further described in the following pages.

(Relationship A) Access Provider to Access Provider

For purposes of this example, consider two access providers. The first is facilities based, owns fiber to the home, and offers an access service such as Gigabit Ethernet. The second access provider is not facilities based and wants to offer a competing Gigabit Ethernet service on a wavelength of its competitor's fiber facility.[81] The interconnection relationship between these two providers is of interest to policy makers to ensure that competition exists in the access markets.

(Relationship B) Access Provider to Transport Provider

These relationships establish the interconnection of the access networks to the backbone service providers as well as to other services. Whether these two providers are actually the same company is irrelevant here. The point is that the end user may wish to make use of different transport providers. This ability to choose should encourage a competitive market.

(Relationship C) Transport Provider to Transport Provider

These relationships establish the interconnected IP transport infrastructure. The relationships are typified by the peering and transit arrangements for traffic exchange that exist among backbone network providers (e.g., WorldCom) and access ISPs (e.g., EarthLink).[82] Application services that these same providers may offer (such as EarthLink's e-mail service) are not included in the transport-to-transport provider relationship. Interdomain QoS interconnections fall into this relationship category as well.

---

81  This example was inspired by research on competition in the last mile by A. Banarjee and M.A. Sirbu at Carnegie Mellon University.

82  M. Kende, "The Digital Handshake: Connecting Internet Backbones" (OPP Working Paper no. 32, Federal Communications Commission, September 2000).

(Relationship D) IP Transport Provider to Application Service Provider

These relationships enable application service providers to access the transport networks that carry their traffic. Examples of these relationships include those between (but are not limited to) the following:

- Transport providers and content providers

- Transport providers and caching/storage providers

- Transport providers, and electronic mail and Web hosting service providers

- Transport providers and new application providers

It is important to recognize that new applications can quickly enter this space and radically change the landscape. Napster is an example of such an application. In less than a year, Napster raised a number of legal, policy, and architectural issues. It is this dynamic nature of the Internet that requires the government to use prudence when considering policy that impacts the Internet.


(Relationship E) Application Service Provider to Application Service Provider

The end-user subset of the application services market sector is characterized by low economies of scale. This factor (together with others) should keep this market sector competitive. Intermediate applications, however—such as those that facilitate end-user applications (e.g., telephony signaling, directory services, caching)—may become important from a public policy perspective if a single provider dominates and has the power to thrive without interconnection to other application service providers.


(Relationship F) Application Service Provider to Content Provider

While in the traditional media outlets, such as television and radio, the large conglomerates dominate the distribution of content; this need not be the case on the Web. This will help keep the content services market competitive. What could potentially become a policy concern is a scenario in which a dominant search engine uses its power to manipulate search results while operating outside the reach of regulation.[83]

(Relationship G) Internet Service Provider to Telecommunications Service Provider

For the foreseeable future, the emerging IP infrastructure needs to interconnect with selected parts of the legacy PSTN infrastructure. With the current regulatory status of Internet services as information services, a telecommunications service provider with market power may be able to erect barriers to entry. These barriers may include restricted access to rights-of-way, restricted access to signaling for call routing and completion, and restricted access to 911/E911 services.[84]

## *Application to Current Issues*

At the time of this writing, *network neutrality* is at the center of a debate between providers of IP transport and access services on one side and providers of both content and application services that consume IP transport services on the other. It is a debate over acceptable forms of service and price discrimination in the market for IP transport services. Providers of the pipe—IP transport and access services—argue that they should have the right to charge more for higher levels of service (higher in terms of bandwidth consumed and/or qualities of service required). Providers of services that fill the pipe—content and application services—argue that such discrimination will threaten innovation and entrepreneurship on the Internet.[85]

In 2002 and 2005, respectively, the FCC reclassified DSL and cable broadband access services as information services. Previously, they had each been classified

---

83    J. Naughton, "Why Google Leaves Just Leaves Everybody Goggling," *London Observer*, January 27, 2002, http://www.observer.co.uk/business/story/0,6903,639855,00. html. This article expresses concern about the growing predominance of the Google search engine. We have also based this viewpoint on a Fall 1999 conversation with M.A. Sirbu.

84    J. Mindel and M. Sirbu, "Regulatory Treatment of IP Transport Services," in *Communications Policy in Transition: The Internet and Beyond* 59 (B.M. Compaine and S. Greenstein, eds. 2001).

85    T. Wu, "Network Neutrality, Broadband Discrimination," *Journal of Telecommunications and High Technology Law* 2 (2005) 141.

as telecommunications services (under Title II regulation). In the language of the layered model we describe in this book, DSL- and cable-model broadband services are now classified as IP transport services.[86, 87]

---

86    Inquiry Concerning High-Speed Access to the Internet Over Cable and Other Facilities, Declaratory Ruling and Notice of Proposed Rulemaking, 17 F.C.C.R. 4798 (2002), upheld in *Nat'l Cable & Telecomm. Ass'n v. Brand X Internet Serv.*, 125 S. Ct. 2688, 2706-08 (2005).

87    Appropriate Framework for Broadband Access to the Internet over Wireline Facilities; Universal Services Obligations of Broadband Providers, Report and Order and Notice of Proposed Rulemaking, FCC 20 FCC Rcd 14853 (2005) (http://ftp. fcc.gov/FCC-05-150A1.pdf).

# 9

# APPENDIX—PROTOCOL TUTORIAL

This appendix provides a brief tutorial on protocols, layering, the TCP/IP protocol suite, and types of standards. This information is intended only as a primer; additional references are provided for the interested reader.

## *Protocols*

With any form of standardized communication, the use of protocols has to be employed. A *protocol* is a well-defined set of rules for intercommunication. The realized benefit of a protocol-based method for communication was around long before the invention of the telephone. In fact, language is a form of a protocol. Both spoken and written language are governed by a well-known set of rules that enables a person to confer his or her ideas to others. Without language to structure one's thoughts, communication of complex ideas would be almost impossible. One of the most important roles of language is to provide a naming convention by which people can abstractly refer to the same concept. For example, when a person hears or reads the word "chair" without the actual object present to be referenced, he or she can be assured that the speaker or author is referring to something that someone can sit on. Without this commonality between the two communicating parties, this form of communication would not be possible.

In electronic communication, protocols and their respective rules have to be even more strictly adhered to. Electronic communication removes the human element from the actual transmission. The human element in both spoken and written language allows meaning to be taken out of context. Thus, even though not every rule (e.g., punctuation, spelling, or pronunciation) is strictly followed, a person is still able to discern the meaning behind the communication. On the other hand, an electronic communication system employs electromagnetic signals over a given medium to transmit information (see Figure 9.1). The endpoints connected to this medium must have a shared set of rules in order to send and receive the information reliably. Since these types of transmissions cannot be taken out of context, these rules must be followed exactly. Consequently, well-defined protocols in electronic communications play an even more important role than in other forms of communication.

**Figure 9.1 Electronic Communication**

## *Layers of Protocols*

In a simple world where there are only two nodes using a single type of application, the needed functionality of the system is minimal. Once the number of nodes and the type of applications are generalized, the needed functionality of the system increases dramatically. The communications system has to be able to differentiate between not only the nodes themselves but also the different applications running at a given node. The added complexity resulting from the increased functionality of the system has made an abstraction of functionality necessary. The end result is a layered architecture where each layer performs a particular task independent of the layers above and below it.

In general, the functionality behind most modern communication systems can be divided into four distinct and independent layers: the application, transport, network, and link access layers. Collectively, these layers are referred to as the *communications stack*. The application layer interprets information into a usable format for the end user. The transport layer helps guarantee that information arrives at the end nodes reliably. The network layer routes information through the network. Lastly, the link access layer exchanges the actual information between nodes.[88] These layers act in a peered relationship across the network via a shared protocol for each layer. For example, the link access layer utilizes link access protocols to share operational information with the link access layer of its peer. The same applies for the network access layer. In the case of the application and trans-

---

88     The link access layer includes the physical layer and the data link layer.

port layers, the peered relationship occurs at the endpoints since they both provide end-to-end functionality (see Figure 9.2).

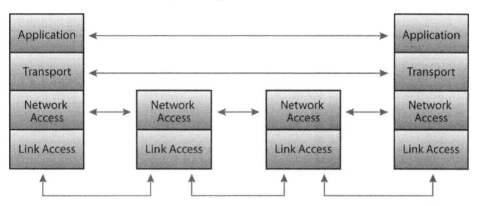

**Figure 9.2 Four Layer Model**

This form of layered architecture provides for a high degree of modularity in system design. As an example, the transport layer can be interchanged throughout
the system without forcing a change to the application layer, network layer, or link
access layer. For a systems engineer, modularization keeps design, implementation, and maintenance of a system tractable. In terms of operation, information
moves down the communications stack at the source and then across the network.
As information moves down the communications stack, each layer adds the relevant information for that layer. This forms the protocol data unit (PDU) for that
layer. Once the information reaches its destination via multiple network access
hops, the information moves up the communications stack at the destination. As
information moves up the communications stack, each layer removes the information relevant to that layer (see Figure 9.3).

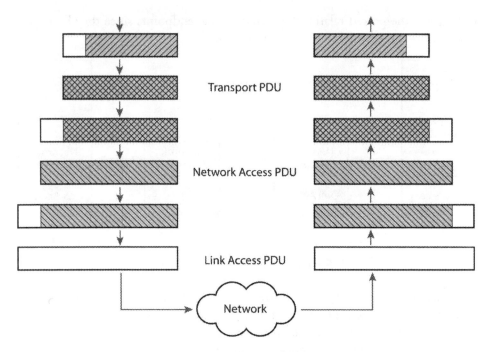

**Figure 9.3 Protocol PDUs**

The communications stack most often used to describe packet-switched network communication is the Open Systems Interconnection (OSI) Reference Model developed by the International Organization for Standardization (ISO). Network engineers began work on the OSI Reference Model in 1978 because of concern over network compatibility. The resultant Reference Model was adopted as an international standard in 1978 (ISO 7498). The Model provides a framework for the development of network interfaces. Unlike the four-layer model described previously, OSI outlines seven layers of functionality:

- *Application (Layer 7):* Provides procedures for accessing OSI services

- *Presentation (Layer 6):* Provides independence from differing presentation formats

- *Session (Layer 5):* Provides management routines for communications control

- *Transport (Layer 4):* Provides transparent end-to-end flow control and error checking

- *Network (Layer 3):* Provides the necessary relaying and routing mechanisms

- *Data Link (Layer 2):* Provides synchronization and error control for a physical link

- *Physical (Layer 1):* Provides the necessary functionality to transmit a raw bit stream across a physical link

Similar to the four-layer model, the lower layers of OSI primarily provide hop-to-hop functionality, whereas the higher layers provide end-to-end functionality (see Figure 9.4).

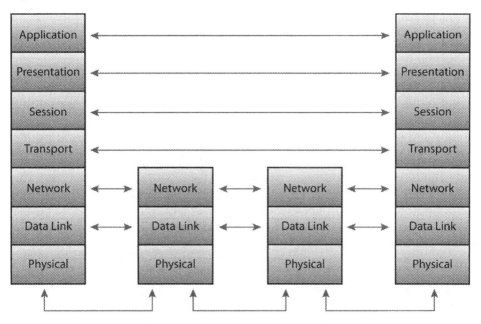

**Figure 9.4 OSI Reference Model**

The designers of the Reference Model intended it to be the predominant blueprint for subsequent network architectures, eventually replacing rival communications stacks. While it did not successfully replace the rival stacks, it did influence their design. Support for the Model was not enough to displace the already mature TCP/IP protocol stack (discussed later in this section). Even though there are very few actual implementations of the Model, most communications stacks use OSI as a descriptive reference for their own functionality.

## PSTN Protocol Layering

Communications in both the PSTN and the Internet are implemented by layers of protocols. Both communications networks can be conceptualized in terms of the OSI Reference Model. It is quite commonplace to think of the Internet in terms of the OSI Reference Model, though the Model can also be applied to the PSTN to facilitate comparison of the two networks.

In the PSTN, the end nodes do not implement all OSI Layers. In fact, the end nodes—or telephone sets—are assumed to be relatively "dumb" and rely on the intervening telephone network to provide the "missing" OSI Layer services. The telephone set and the telephone network provide the application layer service called voice communications. The telephone set provides a Session Layer service through the keypad on which a user dials a telephone number. The telephone set also provides three Physical Layer services: (1) off-hook activates an electrical connection between the telephone set and the switch at the PSTN central office, (2) converts sound (actually air pressure) to electricity to enable transmission of the speaker's voice over the telephone network, and, similarly, (3) converts electricity to air pressure (to create sound) to enable the listener to hear the sounds sent by the speaker at the other end of the telephone conversation. The following diagram depicts the PSTN in terms of the OSI Reference Model, with an emphasis on the fact that most Layer services are provided by the network, not by the telephone set. In the Internet, the end nodes (e.g., computers) implement the full OSI Layer stack of protocols, while the network provides only the bottom three OSI Layers.

POTS on the PSTN uses circuit-switching. Circuit-switching and the PSTN have evolved over the past one hundred years to optimize the handling of voice communications. Circuit-switching involves the establishment of a dedicated communications path between the two communicating nodes; i.e., a circuit is established for the duration of the call. It is dedicated in the sense that no other communicating entities (persons or computers) can utilize that resource while it is reserved, whether or not it is being used. A significant amount of signaling is required to set up and tear down this communications channel. The level of effort to set up and tear down the call, as well as the dedicated communications path, are two key reasons why circuit-switching is wasteful of resources for data transmissions that may involve short, intermittent transmissions of data along a given path. It is more efficient to provide network bandwidth precisely when the communicating entities need it and to make it available to other communicating entities at all other times.

## *Internet or TCP/IP Protocol Layering*

Packet-switching provides network resources on demand, rather than dedicating it, as in circuit-switching. Packet-switching was developed to support the requirements of data networking, and it is now being deployed by the carriers for the carriage of voice and data. Voice carriage in a packet-switched network is made possible by deploying protocols that provide differentiated classes of services that accommodate the unique requirements of voice communications (e.g., delay and jitter minimization).[89] Two significant reasons for the ongoing shift from circuit-switched to packet-switched carrier networks are (1) the emergence of data as the dominant form of traffic on the nation's telecommunications networks and (2) simplified planning and management of a single network for all traffic types.

The TCP/IP protocol suite represents a layered set of protocols. These protocols are developed through an open standards process, mainly under the auspices of the IETF. The TCP/IP protocol suite contains a number of protocols, of which the TCP and the IP represent the foundation. In packet-switching, data is broken into fragments, control information is added to the fragment, and the result is referred to as a *packet*. Network nodes forward the packet through the network. At each node, the packet is stored and the control information is processed. This information provides (among other things) the routing for the packet. The IP describes this routing function in the Internet. There are two basic ways that packets can travel through the network: datagram and virtual circuit. Datagram service requires no initial route setup; rather, the packets travel independently of one another without reliable transmission guarantees. With virtual circuits, a route is established before the actual transmission of data occurs. This route comprises a number of links between source and destination. The TCP describes the specifications that support virtual circuits, whereas UDP defines the datagram service.

TCP is responsible for making sure that the messages get from end to end. It tracks what is sent and received and takes corrective actions when problems arise. On the send side, TCP breaks messages it receives from the application into datagrams. On the receive side, TCP reassembles datagrams back into messages for the receiving application. TCP is also responsible for keeping the datagrams in order (or sequence). TCP accomplishes this task by creating a virtual connection through the network. The traffic follows this path through the network, thereby ensuring the order. TCP sends datagrams to IP. IP is responsible for providing the

---

89    Overprovisioning could also be used; some network designers believe that overprovisioning obviates the need for complex QoS protocols.

information to get the datagram to the destination. IP adds a header that, among other things, adds a source and destination address, correction information, and a protocol number to the datagram. It is at this point that the datagram becomes a packet.

UDP is an alternate protocol to TCP. Unlike TCP, UDP does not provide reliability and packet-ordering guarantees. Without such overhead, UDP is faster and useful with applications that do not require such guarantees. VoIP and streaming media are two applications that use UDP rather than TCP. With VoIP, there is no time to retransmit lost packets, since by the time the retransmitted packet is received at the destination, that part of the phone call has passed.

The IP hierarchy can be described as having an "hourglass" shape, in which a single common protocol that forms the "waist" of the hierarchy supports a variety of application and transport layers above; it then allows a diversity of physical layer transmission and switching services below. The waist provides a uniform address space and service abstraction used for communications between addressable network components.

IP is the "waist" in the Internet. IP addresses are the uniform set of addresses shared by all addressable components of the Internet. The IP datagram service is used for communication. For comparison purposes, it is also useful to apply the hourglass metaphor to the PSTN. As stated in *R&D [Research and Development] Challenges for the National Information* by David Clark and Mark Wegleitner:

> This same hourglass notion applies in part to the Public Switched Telephone Network (PSTN). The PSTN has a global numbering plan and a simple service abstraction, the 3-KHz analog channel. The original application of this channel was limited to human-to-human communication in the beginning but has been extended to support applications like fax and modem transmissions in modern times. At lower layers, the 3-KHz service abstraction has been implemented out of a continually changing set of technologies, from direct analog transmission and switching through today's modem fully digital switched and transmitted ISDN [Integrated Services Digital Network] networks.

As mentioned, in both the Internet and PSTN hourglass models, a great diversity of technologies can be employed below the "waist" of the hourglass to provide transmission and switching services.

## *Open vs. Closed Standards*

There are numerous standards and standards organizations participating in the development of future telecommunications standards. Some standards bodies include the Institute of Electrical and Electronics Engineers (IEEE), the Internet Engineering Task Force (IETF), the International Telecommunications Union (ITU), the American National Standards Institute (ANSI), the Telecommunications Industry Association (TIA), the Alliance for Telecommunications Industry Solutions (ATIS) and its Committee Telecommunications Carrier 1 (T1), and numerous others. The IETF coordinates and oversees the development of protocols for the Internet environment, and it has enjoyed growing popularity and representation of the industry. The ITU tends to focus on European-led telecommunications initiatives, but it has international reach. Moreover, as an arm of the United Nations, it carries the weight of international treaty. ANSI is a U.S.-led standards process with a very broad standards focus that includes telecommunications. TIA and ATIS tend to be driven by the corporate sector that supports these bodies.

Vendors such as IBM and Digital once dominated the computer industry with de facto standards such as their Synchronous Network Architecture (SNA) and DECnet products, respectively. For IBM customers, SNA was the network protocol of choice. Similarly for Digital, DECnet was the protocol of choice. Microsoft's Windows operating system represents another company-based standard. These types of standards are not represented by the open, consensus-driven process of such groups as the IETF.

The difference between open standards and closed standards can be seen in terms of openness, interoperability, market relevance, and other characteristics. An open standard represents a process in which anyone can participate. While there might be a charge associated with participation, the process does not exclude any individuals. On the other hand, a closed standard does not allow everyone to participate. In terms of interoperability, open standards allow all companies to create products that can operate with one another. Finally, in terms of market dominance, a company can use its control of the market to tie products together, thereby furthering the company's dominance. These closed groups are the ones that regulators should watch most closely, since there is a significant chance that they will serve only one part of the industry.

# INDEX

*Note:* page references with a "f" refer to figures on the designated page. Page references with a "t" refer to tables on the designated page.

978-0-595-41307-2
0-595-41307-2